What's up with Catalonia?

"... the causes which impel them to the separation ..."

Edited by Liz Castro
Catalonia Press

What's up with Catalonia?
The causes which impel them to the separation

Translated and edited by Liz Castro
Published by Catalonia Press
http://www.cataloniapress.com
Ashfield, Massachusetts, USA

Cover design: Andreu Cabré © 2013 All rights reserved
Proofreading: Margaret Trejo

ISBN:
Print: 978-1-61150-032-5
EPUB: 978-1-61150-033-2
Kindle: 978-1-61150-034-9

Library of Congress Control Number: 2013901821

Contents

Editor's note

Liz Castro

Ever since I started studying the Catalan language at the University of California at Berkeley in 1985, I have felt an unusual kinship with the Catalan people and an undeniable connectedness with Catalonia. And so, I have been pleased with the increased media coverage after Catalonia's massive pro-independence march of September 11, 2012, while at the same time frustrated with its relatively shallow depth. On November 29, 2012, shortly after Catalonia's snap elections, it occurred to me that with the contribution of Catalan experts, the help of new technologies, the power of social networks, and some good translating, I might be able to edit a comprehensive collection of articles so that people outside of Catalonia could get a much clearer idea of just what's going on there. The product of that effort is the book you have before you.

All of the articles were written in December 2012 and January 2013 in an attempt to capture the *current* situation in Catalonia. There is one particularly significant event that happened just after the book was completed: on January 23rd, the Parliament of Catalonia voted in favor of a Declaration of Sovereignty. The process continues to move forward.

The book's subtitle "*...the causes which impel them to the separation...*" is a direct quote from the United States Declaration of Independence, which is also featured on the cover.

Some of the writers who contributed articles for this book I knew previously, but others put their trust in me sight unseen. I am indebted to both groups for their confidence, their collaboration, and their insights. I hope I have captured the spirit of their articles with my translations.

A few notes: many Catalans prefer to refer to Spain as the *Spanish State*, since they consider it an administrative, and not a national, construct. I have followed their example here. I give place names in English if there is an existing translation (that is not simply Spanish), and Catalan when there isn't. The concept of Catalonia and the Catalan Countries is so complex that there is an entire article about it (Vicent Sanchis).

For ongoing coverage of Catalonia's journey toward independence, you can follow me on Twitter (@lizcastro) or read my blog, News Catalonia (http://www.newscatalonia.com). Catalonia Press has published two other excellent books in English on Catalonia: Toni Strubell and Lluís Brunet's beautifully photographed collection of interviews of leading Catalan personalities, *What Catalans Want: Could Catalonia be Europe's Next State?*, and Matthew Tree's collection of essays on life in Barcelona, *Barcelona, Catalonia: The View from the Inside*. Both are available in print and electronic editions. I also highly recommend following the Col·lectiu Emma (Emma Network: http://www.collectiuemma.cat/) and the Wilson Initiative (http://www.wilson.cat/en/), both of which offer excellent English-language stories and articles about Catalonia's independence movement.

Thanks to Andreu Cabré for a fabulous cover, and to Margaret Trejo for proofreading and corrections. Thanks also to the kind folks who already follow me on Twitter who helped with translations and clarifications, sent me information and encouragement, and listened as I told them, in 140 characters at a time, what was happening in Catalonia.

Finally, I would especially like to thank all of the people who supported this book through our crowdsourcing campaign (http://www.verkami.com/projects/4146-what-x27-s-up-with-catalonia), and whose names can be found on Catalonia Press' website: http://www.cataloniapress.com). Many of them sponsored sending a copy of this book to a friend, library, journalist, newspaper, or politician outside of Catalonia, in order to share around the world a more precise picture of just what's up with Catalonia. Catalans are not waiting for anyone to rescue them, but they'll be happy if you know what's going on there. Next time you visit lovely Barcelona, I hope you'll take a long look around, and have a clearer view of the country you're in.

Prologue: A new path for Catalonia

Artur Mas i Gavarró
President of Catalonia

Catalonia is at a historic crossroads, our most exciting and significant moment in many years. There is a lot of excitement around building our country. A country that in part will be new. It is an immense, collective project that involves us all. It won't be an easy road, it'll be steep, and the process will be full of difficulties and obstacles, but, if we stick together and if we persevere, we can make it.

Catalonia, our country, is a nation. A nation that, in order to maintain its identity and to move forward, needs tools of state. This nation has existed for many centuries. It has its own identity, culture, and language, and its own institutions. Catalonia wants to follow, and indeed must be allowed to follow, its own path.

It has been thirty years since we in Catalonia have been doing our best to collaborate with the Spanish State in order to build a democratic, modern, European Spain. We have repeatedly tried to help transform the State to make it ours. We had hoped that Spain would be understanding, tolerant, and above all, respectful of Catalonia's personality, of its culture and its language, and of the hopes for progress and well-being of the Catalan people.

But what do we find has been the answer from the State over these past three decades? We find that we contribute a huge amount, too much even, and that though we help as much as we can, we are neither understood nor respected for who we are. We find ourselves with an immutable annual fiscal deficit of 16 billion euros between what we bring to the State each year and what we receive. We find that our jurisdiction is continually violated, that some debts are recognized but never paid, while other debts are not even recognized. We find a ruling of the Spanish Constitutional Court that is contrary to the Statute of Autonomy approved by the Parliament of Catalonia in 2006. And we find, finally, a categorical NO in response to our proposal of a fiscal pact, approved by our Parliament, in a last attempt to seek a fairer agreement, more fitting of equal partners, on the difference between our monetary contribution to the State and what it gives back. That proposal neither broke nor lessened our commitment to solidarity with the other territories of the State, but nevertheless we were told that there was no margin for negotiation.

In that context, on September 11, 2012, on Catalonia's National Day, there was a massive demonstration, in which 1.5 million people—that is, a fifth of our population—demanded that Catalonia become a new State in Europe. This huge demonstration came on the heels of the march that took place on July 10, 2010, with the slogan, "We are a nation. We decide." shortly after the Constitutional Court's ruling against Catalonia's Statute of 2006.

What's up with Catalonia, then? What is up is that this hope of making Spain our State and having them respect our personality, our aspirations, our culture, and our language has been frustrated and a significant majority of the people of Catalonia have said that they wish to begin a new path. We have realized that in the same way that Spain went through its transition thirty years ago, it is now time for Catalonia to go through its own national transition. This is the only path open to us that will allow us to achieve a collective well-being that is commensurate with our productive capacity; social justice that relies more on the autonomous decisions of Catalan institutions and the shared values of the Catalan people; and a cultural identity that we can project around the world.

In concrete terms, national transition means giving the people a voice so that they can freely decide their own future. We want to center our national transition on the right to self-determination—based on sovereignty and democracy—which we have to face with a peaceful spirit, with a solid majority, and at the same time, with abundant respect for the minority.

Catalonia is living exceptional moments and it needs exceptional decisions. For that reason, I decided to hold snap elections in order to let the people have their say. I proposed that in this legislature we would hold a referendum where the Catalan people can freely and peacefully decide their future as a nation.

This is the new central issue in Catalonia. A Catalonia that suffers, like the rest of the countries in Europe, the harsh consequences of the financial crisis, that suffers the consequences of having to drastically reduce its public spending to meet the deficit objectives that are disproportionately, unjustly, and disloyally imposed by Spain, and that suffers the consequences of having to shoulder the return of a debt of massive dimensions. It faces this difficult and complex situation without any of the tools that states have at their disposal, and with the growing sensation that the state that we helped to construct neither protects us, nor defends us, nor respects us.

The lack of instruments and tools keeps us from being able to respond satisfactorily to our people's problems, despite the fact that we have the necessary capacity and resources to meet the current challenges. We must have the power to decide if we want to be responsible for our own decisions and if we want to continue within a state that wants to minimize our nationhood, stymie our economic growth, and interfere with the maintenance of our well-being.

Therefore, during the legislature that has just begun in Catalonia, we Catalans will be called to the polls to be consulted on our political and national future. This referendum will be held within a legal framework and with the explicit desire of arriving at the widest consensus possible among all the political and social forces in the country. At the same time as we prepare the referendum, the Government of Catalonia will work to define and develop the structures of state that we must have at the ready for this new scenario. We will also dedicate our efforts to explaining to Europe and the world the democratic process that we have begun and to make very clear that what we aspire to is simply to be a normal country in the European Union.

In Catalonia, we are facing crucial, momentous, and vital turning points in our history and we do so convinced that it will lead us to a better country. It is our duty and our responsibility to leave to future generations a country of which they can feel very proud.

Catalonia, a new state in Europe

Carme Forcadell Lluís

Degrees in Philosophy and Communication Sciences from the Autonomous University of Barcelona and Masters in Catalan Philology. Professor of Secondary Teacher Education. Since 1985, Forcadell has worked in the Department of Education, as coordinator of linguistic normalization for the Catalan Teaching Service and currently as consultant on language, interculturalism, and social cohesion for the Western Vallès area. She has published several books on pedagogy, together with other authors, as well as a dictionary. She has written for several media publications. She has been active over the years in various organizations and is currently the president of the Catalan National Assembly.

Since September 11, 1714, as a consequence of a military defeat, Catalonia has formed part of the Kingdom of Spain. And each September 11 we commemorate our National Day, not to remember our defeat, but on the contrary, to remember that despite the defeat, and the subsequent suffering and the attempts to wipe us out, we continue to exist. During the almost 300 years that Catalonia has lived as part of the Spanish State, we have tried several times to recover our national freedoms that we lost by force of arms, but it hasn't been until now, in the 21st century, that we have had the political, social, cultural, and economic conditions necessary to achieve independence.

On September 11, 2012, more than 1.5 million people came out on the streets of Barcelona to demonstrate behind a placard that read *Catalonia: New State in Europe*. A demonstration of 1.5 million people in a country of 7.5 million inhabitants can easily be qualified as one of the largest, if not the largest, in history. And if we add to this the fact that the demonstration was celebrated in an absolutely democratic and peaceful manner, and that it was convoked by the civil society, it is even more extraordinary.

This demonstration was in fact convoked and organized by the Catalan National Assembly (ANC), an entity formed by people of various ideologies and different social classes that pursue a common objective: the independence of Catalonia. We plan to dissolve once we have achieved our goal. The Assembly was formally constituted six months before the demonstration, on March 10, 2012, even though we were working on this project a full two years earlier. I was invited to join by Miquel Strubell, one of the founders of the Assembly, when there were only 20 members.

From the very beginning, we were clear that the goal of the ANC was to achieve Catalonia's independence, and thus the only thing that we had to decide was how and when. To do so, we elaborated a road map which explained the steps necessary for reaching our goal. One of the first proposals that emerged was organizing a demonstration on September 11, Catalonia's National Day, or *Diada*. We wanted to have a different kind of *Diada*, where for the first time the independentist political parties and the civic organizations could come together in a joint demonstration, instead of everyone having their own separate ones, as in previous years.

We knew that the demonstration had to be unified, massive, and peaceful and that we had to get all the parties and organizations together that were in favor of creating our own state in order to show the strength of our national objective, both to ourselves and to the world. The Government of Catalonia publicly asked that our demonstration be in support of the fiscal pact—an economic proposal that they were trying to negotiate that very month with the Spanish government. The ANC decided against the request. We had already decided that we would only come out to demand independence, we had already approved such an act in our constituent assembly—it was part of our road map—and we were convinced that that was what the people of Catalonia wanted.

It was important that once September 11 was over, the message in favor of independence would remain clear and convincing. We needed to show the world that we wanted our own state and we could only do so if we remained firm in our objective of having a demonstration with the lemma that everyone had already agreed on. We knew that the demonstration was going to be very important because from all over the country we were getting reports that they were filling up buses for Barcelona. There were so many enthusiastic and hopeful people in all of our meetings held to explain why we wanted independence and to invite people to march with us. Our intuition told us the march would be very successful.

Even so, we worried about the turnout. It was important that it be a significant march, the biggest one in Catalonia's history. Even though there had already been very large marches in Barcelona—always to defend our national rights—this one had to be even bigger. We had to demonstrate that a majority of Catalans were in favor of independence. Our other worry and, indeed my biggest worry, was guaranteeing the safety of all of the marchers. Everything had to be peaceful and festive. We knew that if there were any incidents, the goal of the march would be blurred, and the image that would be seen and that the world would remember would be that of violent incidents or counter-demonstrators. But our fears were unfounded. Everything turned out as we hoped, and the Catalan people proved its great maturity and civility.

We had written a letter to the president of the Government and to the president of the Parliament asking that we be received at the end of the march so that we could share with them our road map, whose most important milestone was our proposal to hold a referendum in which the Catalan people could decide its own future. Only the president of the Parliament agreed to meet us after the demonstration. However, we knew that if the march was important enough, the president of the Government would also meet with us, if not that same day, then soon after. That's exactly what happened.

Two days later we met with President Artur Mas and had a very cordial meeting. We explained that we were happy to work toward independence and to support the Government as long as they showed that they were also in favor of working toward having a sovereign state. The president explained that he had made a previous commitment together with the Catalan Parliament to go to Madrid to speak with the president of the Spanish government, in order to negotiate a fiscal pact, in an attempt to end the fiscal plundering that Catalonia has suffered for many years.

For the ANC, the trip to Madrid didn't make any sense. We considered it a waste of time, but we respected the president's decision. We spoke for a long time about the timeline that should be dedicated to these negotiations before continuing our demands and demonstrations in favor of a sovereign state. All of us believed that President Rajoy, the president of the Spanish government, would ask for time to study the proposal and the ANC didn't want this period of time to drag out more than two months. Luckily for us, Mr. Rajoy roundly refused to negotiate a fair fiscal agreement for Catalonia and this clear refusal changed our history by pushing President Mas—who already felt pressured by the march and without any viable alternative that justified continuing the government—to convoke snap elections, which would be celebrated two months later, on November 25.

These were elections in which the political parties had to make their positions clear, since the people were demanding to know where each party stood, if they were in favor or if they were against having a referendum on the independence of Catalonia. During these elections, the people of Catalonia again demonstrated that they wanted a sovereign state—the first and second most voted parties in the elections are in favor—and now we have a Government that is committed to holding a referendum. The Catalan National Assembly is committed to supporting the government in holding a referendum. We will continue to work on our road map that, now that the Government has taken on the goal of having a referendum, is especially focused on widening the social majority in favor of independence. If necessary, we will return to the streets to continue our struggle in favor of the freedom of our people.

In Catalonia, we are living one of the most exhilarating years in our history. It will be a hard, difficult, complicated year, because we are suffering a financial crisis together with the rest of Southern Europe, exacerbated by the economic asphyxiation that Catalonia suffers at the hands of the Spanish government. Despite everything, we Catalans are excited and hopeful for the future because, for the first time, we are in reach of a dream that so many Catalans share: that we can recover the freedom that we lost almost 300 years ago. The Spanish State has said that we cannot hold a referendum, that we cannot decide our own future because it is illegal, because the Spanish laws don't allow it. Indeed, many of these Spanish laws, the Constitution included, were made expressly so that Catalans could not decide our own future. They were created to suppress the minority.

For the Catalan National Assembly, the arguments of the Spanish State against celebrating a referendum have no validity. Laws can be changed. Indeed, if they could not be changed, women would still not be allowed to vote, because that too was once illegal. Laws must be at the service of the people. Democracy is above individual laws.

Catalonia is a Mediterranean country, between Spain and France, that wants to decide its future in a completely democratic and peaceful way, just as we have demonstrated to the world. Our perseverance and will to exist are so strong that even after 300 years of domination our dreams of liberty remain strong and steadfast. We want to become one of the free people of the world and we are confident that we can achieve that goal with the support of the other people in the world who in their own time were able to achieve their own goals of independence and their own dream of freedom.

2013: The transition year toward the referendum on independence

Oriol Junqueras

President of Esquerra Republicana de Catalunya [Republican Left of Catalonia], MP, and Leader of the Opposition in the Parliament of Catalonia. Mayor of Sant Vicenç dels Horts. B.A. in Modern and Contemporary History, Ph.D. in History of Economic Thought. Until 2012 Professor at Autonomous University of Barcelona. Member of European Parliament between July 2009 and December 2011, as an independent candidate from ERC, and head of the European Free Alliance coalition in Spain.

On November 25, 2012, Catalonia celebrated what we hope will be our last "Autonomous Community" elections. We have arrived at this point after the largest demonstration that Catalonia has ever seen, with a million and a half Catalans marching in the streets of Barcelona, demanding independence and their will to have their own state within the framework of the European Union and the international community.

During the entire electoral campaign, Esquerra Republicana de Catalunya, the Republican Left of Catalonia, the country's oldest party—founded in 1931—and the one that has historically defended the independence of Catalonia, insisted on the plebiscitary character of the election, and on how important it was for Catalans to vote so that on the day after the election, nobody might negotiate away their dreams for freedom that at that moment, after the march, seemed more real than ever before.

And they listened. The result of the November 25 election made it essential for those of us who believe in a sovereign Catalonia to get along. The mandate from the polls was crystal clear: There must be joint leadership toward the right to self-determination and, at the same time, an application of economic alternatives that are more fair and more effective at getting us out of the financial crisis. And that is, in so many words, the goal of the pact agreed on by the two principal parties in Catalonia: CiU (Convergència i Unió), which with 50 seats in Parliament is by far the most voted party in the country, and Esquerra, which with 21 seats is the second force, and the Leader of the Opposition.

We are convinced that in a crucial moment like this one, where the difficulties of a profound financial crisis coincide with the most important process that a nation can undertake—that of becoming a state—we must have a strong government, which can only result from having solid parliamentary support behind the most important key decisions facing the country. For that reason, the major agreements consist of, on the one hand, confronting the financial crisis with fiscal policies that reduce the budget cuts by establishing new taxes in sectors that still have an ability to pay: banks, nuclear power plants, large estates, and large commercial ventures.

On the other hand, we have agreed on the steps necessary for celebrating a Referendum on Independence in 2014. These steps, which are to be carried out during 2013, will make it possible for us to be ready to celebrate the referendum in 2014. This means finding and guaranteeing the legal framework in which such a referendum can occur, whether that be Catalan, Spanish, or international law, and at the same time negotiating the terms with which the referendum will be held, like Scotland and the United Kingdom are doing, for example.

At the same time, it's crucial that this agreement continue to evolve and that it be open to the other political groups in the Catalan Parliament, and even more important, to the whole of Catalan society: unions, employers, universities, community groups, organizations, and so on. In fact, in order to successfully get through the enormous difficulties that lie ahead in the coming months and make it to the referendum, we will need a compact, a commitment of the whole country that allows us to draw up common plans for the future.

This same compact will need to illustrate the link between a timely recovery from the financial crisis and specific policies and investments that allow us to restore public spending and investments, to defend, improve, and expand the welfare state, to create active policies for economic growth and for job creation, and that at the same time, allow us to progressively reverse an important portion of the budget cuts that have been applied up to this point. It makes no sense to develop these plans for the future as a quick, temporary fix simply because there are many elements that don't depend directly on us but rather on an international context and on the Spanish government and, therefore, they must instead be substantial and substantiated.

We are sure that the bulk of the country is in favor of working out the framework of such a compact, of this major agreement, and that in any case, it is worth our efforts. Indeed, it may be that the very act of communicating our road map, our plans for the future, to our citizens is the necessary element for engendering confidence among them in a moment in which confidence and certainty with respect to the economic future is in short supply.

Many of our fellow citizens have been unable to find work for much too long, some of them have lost their jobs recently, and others fear losing their employment in the near future. Some are facing difficult issues in their family situations, with their children's schools, or with healthcare. These people will surely appreciate the increased confidence and will also put a part of their faith in the work that we are all trying to do together. These people all deserve and need to know that we elected representatives will do everything possible to construct these key major agreements and that we are committed to dedicating ourselves, to strengthening our efforts, and to persevering in linking the recovery of our government's income to policies that defend, improve, and expand the welfare state, to reactivate our economy, and to promote job creation.

In the next few months, the future of our country will be in the balance, and we will need a good dose of serenity, firmness, strength, and constancy in order to direct Catalonia's destiny to a good end. The challenge is enormous and the opportunity is extraordinary.

Premeditated asphyxia

Elisenda Paluzie

Professor at the University of Barcelona since 2001 and dean of the School of Economics and Business since 2009. Paluzie holds a M.Sc. in International and Development Economics from Yale University (1996) and a Ph.D. in Economics from the University of Barcelona (1999). She has published papers in journals, reports, and books on international trade, economic geography, Catalan fiscal flows, and the regional financing system.

Catalonia might appear to the external eye as a selfish region trying to avoid its duties toward poor regions in a time of distress. To a great majority of its population, the feeling is more similar to that of an exhausted cash-cow, tired of paying Swedish-level taxes in exchange for sub-par public services, and of being made a scapegoat for the debt crisis in Spain, to boot. The current state of the Catalan government's finances are the consequence of a premeditated asphyxia just as was predicted by the late public finance professor and former Catalan treasury minister, Ramon Trias Fargas, all the way back in 1985. Let's take a look.

Since the transition process to democracy in the late seventies, Spain has been organized as a decentralized state. It is not a federal country, but there is an important degree of political decentralization. The country is composed of seventeen *autonomous communities*, each one with its own parliament and some degree of legislative power. The fiscal decentralization model is asymmetric: there are two systems, the *common* and the *foral* regimes.

Under the "foral" regime, the Basque Country and Navarre are governed by an Economic Agreement ("Concierto" and "Convenio", respectively), which gives each the power to collect and manage its entire tax system. The contribution of the Basque Country to the central government to cover statewide expenditures is called the "cupo"; and that of Navarre, the "cuota". Hence these autonomous communities have fiscal sovereignty.

The common regime regulates the tax system of the other fifteen autonomous communities, including Catalonia, and is basically a decentralized unitarian model which has evolved over time, characterized by high expenditure decentralization but low fiscal sovereignty over revenues. Tax sharing and transfers are the keystones of this model.

Under the common regime an important process of inter-regional redistribution has taken place over time. To measure the degree of regional redistribution, net fiscal flows (the difference between the revenues collected in a region and government direct spending in the region) are calculated. If the net fiscal flow of a region is negative, we say that the region has a *fiscal deficit*. If it is positive the region runs a *fiscal surplus*. Catalonia's fiscal deficit has increased over time and is on average around 8 percent of Catalan GDP, a figure that is particularly large by international standards. While as a relatively rich region (the fourth in GDP per capita), Catalonia's net transfers to other regions could be understandable, its magnitude is not at all reasonable. Table 1 shows the fiscal balances of all Spanish autonomous communities in 2005 by the cash-flow approach as calculated by the Instituto de Estudios

Fiscales (Institute of Fiscal Studies), an institution linked to the Spanish Treasury. According to these estimates the fiscal deficit of Catalonia is considerable (almost 9 percent of the Catalan GDP and 15 billion euros in 2005).

Table 1. Regional net fiscal flows, 2005

	Cash-flow approach (million Euros)	Cash-flow approach (in % GDP)	Ranking GDP per capita
1. Balearic Islands	– 3,191	– 14.2	7
2. Catalonia	– 14,808	– 8.7	4
3. Valencia	– 5,575	– 6.3	13 (below average)
4. Madrid	– 8,911	– 5.6	1
5. Navarre	– 488	– 3.2	3
6. Murcia	– 499	– 2.1	15 (below average)
7. Basque Country	– 758	– 1.3	2
8. La Rioja	+ 44	+ 0.7	6 (above average)
9. Canary Islands	+ 590	+ 1.6	14
10. Aragon	+ 510	+ 1.8	5 (above average)
11. Castile-la Mancha	+ 1,103	+ 3.5	17
12. Andalusia	+ 5,729	+ 4.5	18
13. Cantabria	+ 571	+ 5.0	8 (above average)
14. Castile-Leon	+ 3,692	+ 7.6	11
15. Galicia	+ 3,807	+ 8.2	16
16. Asturias	+ 2,780	+ 14.3	12
17. Extremadura	+ 2,695	+ 17.8	19
18. Ceuta	+ 388	+ 28.6	9
19. Melilla	+ 421	+ 34.0	10

Source: Instituto de Estudios Fiscales, Ministerio de Economía y Hacienda (2008).

Catalonia is the fourth community in GDP per capita, the Balearic Islands the seventh, and Valencia the thirteenth, but these three autonomous communities occupy the top three places in the ranking by fiscal deficit. There are regions with a GDP per capita higher than the Spanish average such as Aragon, Cantabria, and La Rioja, which show a fiscal surplus. The system does not seem to follow a rational pattern. The case of Valencia is paradigmatic: this region has a GDP per capita below the Spanish average (89 percent) and has a fiscal deficit that attains 6.3 percent of its GDP.

The most recent estimates are available only for Catalonia and have been calculated by the Catalan government. On average, in the period 2002–2009,

Catalonia had a fiscal deficit of 8.6 percent of its GDP. In 2009, the last year in the series, it amounted to 16.4 billion euros, that is, 2,251 euros per capita.

Another way to look at this data is in relative terms, as compared to total income and expenditures of the Spanish government. Thus, during the period 2002–2009, Catalonia provided 19.55 percent of all central government and Social Security income in Spain while receiving only 13.5 percent of all central government and Social Security expenditures. If we exclude personal redistribution, channeled through Social Security (social contributions, pensions, and unemployment benefits), the figures are more extreme. Catalonia contributed 19.7 percent to central government income, and received only 10.31 percent of central government expenditures. This means that for each euro paid in taxes to the central government, only 52 cents return to Catalonia, while 48 cents are not spent in Catalonia.

The origin of this large fiscal deficit is twofold. On the one hand, Spain's government spends little in Catalonia, particularly on infrastructures, and on the other the Catalan government, which is responsible for providing education, health, and social services, has systematically been underfinanced.

Let's first take a look at the central government investment in infrastructures. Figure 1 shows the percentage of central government investment in Catalonia during the period 1999–2013. This percentage has consistently been lower than the ratio of Catalan GDP to Spanish GDP (18.8 percent) and even lower than the ratio of Catalan population to Spanish population (15.4 percent in 1999, 16 percent in 2012).

Figure 1. Central government investment in Catalonia (percent over Spanish total), 1999–2013

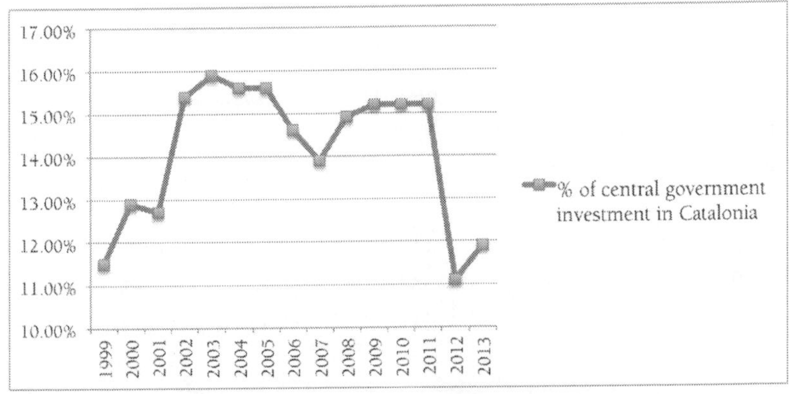

Source: Presupuestos Generales del Estado (Spanish National Budget), several years.

This situation led to the inclusion of a special provision in the 2006 Statute of Autonomy that forced the central government to ensure that for seven years (2007–2013) investment in infrastructure would be commensurate with relative GDP. An agreement was reached between the Catalan and the Spanish governments on the methodology adopted to calculate investments. This methodology excluded some infrastructures from the calculus, but spelled out the obligation of the central government to make a payment to the Catalan government three years later, if the investments had not been executed.

A second objective of the reform of the Catalan Statute of Autonomy in 2005 was a new financing system for the Catalan government. The project of reform approved by the Catalan Parliament originally included a system similar to the Basque "Concierto". However, the Spanish Parliament rewrote those terms and maintained Catalonia in the common regime. Nevertheless, the new Statute of Autonomy was approved in a referendum by the Catalan population in June 2006. It led to the reform of the whole Spanish regional financing system in July 2009. Like previous reforms, the 2009 reform increased tax revenue sharing and maintained the status quo, preventing any region from decreasing revenues. All regions increased their revenues thanks to the additional funds contributed by the central government (11.4 billion euros). The reform increased the regional share of the personal income tax and the VAT up to 50 percent and that of the excise taxes up to 58 percent. But it is important to bear in mind that the tax sharing system still did not include collection and regulation powers.

The Equalization Fund (formerly called the Sufficiency Fund), was split into two new funds: the Essential Public Services Fund, a horizontal transfer, whose purpose is to guarantee the same resources per adjusted capita to all regions for the provision of health, education, and social services; and the Global Sufficiency Fund, whose purpose is to guarantee the status quo clause. In addition, the reform also created two brand new so-called *convergence funds*, meant to compensate two very different types of regions: the Cooperation Fund for the poorest or less dense regions; and the Competitiveness Fund for the regions that would obtain less than average revenues per adjusted capita after the application of the redistribution system.

The gains obtained by Catalonia in 2009, the first year of the reform, amounted to a little less than 2 billion euros, that is, just 1 percent of Catalan GDP (which in 2009 was 195 billion euros). Of these, 937 million euros were obtained through the Competitiveness Fund. In 2010, 863 million euros came from this fund and an additional 465 million euros were provided through the Essential Public Services Fund, totaling an amelioration of 2.3 billion euros.

Thus, the reform didn't significantly reduce Catalonia's fiscal deficit. Moreover, it failed to solve some of the problems of the regional financial system, namely the overequalization problem. Equalization schemes aimed at providing regions with comparable services have been established. Yet, the political economy literature has recently noted that complete equalization might induce richer regions to separate, while a system of partial equalization that reduces the gap between advantaged and disadvantaged regions without completely eliminating it, guarantees the country stability (Le Breton and Weber, 2003; Haimanko, Le Breton and Weber, 2005).

Table 2 shows regional fiscal capacity, before and after equalization in 2010. The Spanish regional financing system clearly overequalizes. Catalonia ranks third in regional fiscal capacity (taxes transferred or shared) before equalization and tenth after equalization. Moreover, not only is Catalonia's order in the ranking not maintained but it also receives below-average funding.

Table 2. Regional fiscal capacity before and after equalization, 2010

	Before equalization		After equalization
1. Madrid	133.3	1. Cantabria	122.8
2. Balearic Islands	122.9	2. Extremadura	119.4
3. Catalonia	118.5	3. La Rioja	117.6
4. Aragon	114.8	4. Castile-Leon	117.1
5. Cantabria	114.0	5. Aragon	113.4
6. Asturias	105.2	6. Asturias	112.9
7. La Rioja	102.3	7. Galicia	111.6
8. Castile-Leon	101.2	8. Castile-La Mancha	104.4
9. Valencia	93.9	9. Balearic Islands	99.8
10. Galicia	90.5	10. Catalonia	98.9
11. Castile-La Mancha	86.6	11. Andalusia	94.5
12. Murcia	84.0	12. Madrid	94.4
13. Andalusia	81.0	13. Valencia	93.5
14. Extremadura	76.4	14. Murcia	93.1
15. Canary Islands	42.1	15. Canary Islands	88.6
Total	100.0	Total	100.0

Source: Ministerio de Economía y Hacienda (2012).

In addition, many problems are linked to the absence of effective tax collecting powers. The central government directly collects 90 percent of the taxes included in the regional financing system. They are transferred to the Catalan government through advances and two years later a settlement is made. This situation generates uncertainty about the effective income that the Catalan government has with which to finance its budget. Collection forecasts were overvalued in 2008 and 2009, hence Catalonia's government should give back 2.5 billion euros to the central government. Moreover, in the recent past, the central government has acted arbitrarily when deciding on the advances that would be made to the autonomous communities. For instance, in 2009 and 2010 advances on the Competitiveness Fund (which delivers half of the benefits of the new financing system for Catalonia) were made, while in 2011 and 2012 the government decided not to advance this fund and pay it two years later. This was particularly painful in those two years when fiscal consolidation implied tight public deficit targets, and in fact, it was a way of diverting public deficit away from the central government and toward the Catalan government.

Moreover, the central government did not make the required transfers according to the agreement in the provision of the Statute of Autonomy on infrastructures. These debts amounted to 759 million euros for the infrastructures not executed in 2008, 211 million euros for those of 2009, and 719 million euros for those of 2010. Thus, in 2013 more than 1.7 billion euros are owed to the Catalan government for these items.

Finally, another matter of heated debate has been the sharing of the fiscal deficit objectives between different government branches. When the EU relaxed the deficit objectives for 2013, and a new goal of 4.5 percent of GDP was established for Spain, the central government distributed the objective as follows: 3.8 percent of GDP for the central government and 0.7 percent of the GDP for the autonomous communities. The Catalan Minister of Economy, Andreu Mas-Colell, has argued that given that regional spending is one third of total spending, a reasonable allocation would be one third for the region and two thirds for the central administration. This would represent a deficit objective of 1.5 percent for the region and 3 percent for the central government. In Catalonia, a deficit target of 0.7 percent of GDP for 2013 implies a huge primary surplus target. (Since interest payments in 2013 will be 2.2 billion euros and 0.7 percent of GDP is about 1.4 billion euros, that means the *primary surplus*—that is, the difference between spending and tax revenues, not counting interest payments—would be around 800 million euros.) In the current recession, this level of rigor is foolish and would put Catalonia in a much more precarious situation than the U.S. fiscal cliff.

The conflict in the relationship between Catalonia and Spain is not just a matter of economics. However, their economic relationship is symptomatic of their broader relationship, characterized by domination, treachery, and a lack of respect by the dominant nation toward the one that was conquered three hundred years ago.

References

Departament d'Economia i Finances (2009) *Metodologia i càlcul de la balança fiscal de Catalunya amb l'administració central 2002–2005.* Grup de Treball per a l'actualització de la balança fiscal de Catalunya. *Monografies*, núm. 10.

Haimanko, O., Le Breton, M. and Weber, S. (2005) "The stability threshold and two facts of polarization", CEPR Discussion Papers No. 5098, CEPR, London, UK.

Le Breton, M. and Weber, S. (2003) "The art of making everybody happy: how to prevent a secession", *IMF Staff Papers* Vol. 50, No.3.

Ministerio de Economía y Hacienda (2012) Liquidación de los recursos del sistema e financiación de las comunidades autónomas de régimen común y ciudades con estatuto de autonomía y de las participaciones en los fondos de convergencia autonómica, regulados en la Ley 22/2009, de 18 de diciembre, correspondientes al ejercicio 2010.

Trias Fargas, Ramon (1985) *Narració d'una asfíxia premeditada. Les finances de la Generalitat de Catalunya.* Reprinted in 2011. Editorial Afers, València.

It's always been there

F. Xavier Vila

Associate professor at the University of Barcelona. Vila obtained an Extraordinary Degree Award in Catalan Philology in Barcelona and a Ph.D. in Linguistics at the Vrije Universiteit Brussel. He was the first director of the CRUSCAT Research Network on sociolinguistics and is the current director of the University Centre for Sociolinguistics and Communication at the University of Barcelona (CUSC-UB). He has published a wide range of books and specialized articles in the areas of sociolinguistics, demolinguistics, and language policy, among them Survival and Development of Language Communities. Prospects and challenges *(Multilingual Matters, 2012).*

When visitors arrive at any of Catalonia's airports, they soon realize they are welcome not in two languages, as in most European cities, but in three: English, Spanish, and Catalan. At first glance, they may be tempted to believe that this presence of Catalan is just a benevolent concession to local pride. But during their trip to the hotel, newcomers rapidly perceive that this is not the case. In fact, most written information, from commercial posters to traffic signs, including all place names, street names, and so on, are written at least, and very often exclusively, in Catalan. Of course, at the hotel, they may be served in several languages, most restaurants offer a multilingual menu, and a very large percentage of the music heard on the radio consists of international hits. Spanish-speaking visitors will manage to communicate in this language with virtually everybody they encounter. But if the visitors keep alert and look beyond this initial curtain, they will soon see how a complex, fascinating, linguistic landscape is slowly revealed before their eyes. Catalan is a crucial piece of this idiomatic puzzle.

In fact, if our visitors leave the hotel and start listening to people on the street, they will soon realize that a large percentage of them speak Catalan to each other. Most immigrants from outside Catalonia communicate either in Spanish—in Castilian, as the language has always been called here—or in their own languages, so don't expect to hear Catalan on every corner in the neighborhoods where Andalusian, Latino, or Moroccan immigrants settled during the last decades. But although locals are at least bilingual and willing to accommodate speakers of other languages, immigration has not led locals to give up Catalan. On the contrary, Catalans use it in all societal domains, from home to the parliament, on the playgrounds, at work, and in the hospitals. Catalan is the main language of instruction in all schools and universities, and it is used by scientists to do research as well as by caretakers to help elderly people. It is the first language used in the Barcelona Football Club stadium, but also in the Liceu, Barcelona's opera house, and in all museums as well. It is the language of most local theater productions, that of hundreds of music bands, and used by the two most followed radio stations (and by many others). Catalan finds itself among the 20 most used languages on the internet, and there's a Catalan version of several widespread software applications such as Windows, Office, YouTube, and Twitter. Not everybody in Catalonia masters Catalan: according to data from the official EULP poll (*Enquesta d'usos lingüístics de la població* [Linguistic usage poll]) in 2008, 94.6 percent of the residents older than 14 years declared they could understand it, while 78.3 percent could speak it, 81.7 percent could read it, and 61.8

percent could write it. But take into account that Catalonia is a society of immigrants. In the sample, as in society as a whole, only 58 percent of the respondents were born in Catalonia, 24 percent elsewhere in Spain—mostly in Castilian-speaking regions—and 17 percent abroad.

Figure 1. Languages used with grandparents, parents, and children in Catalonia

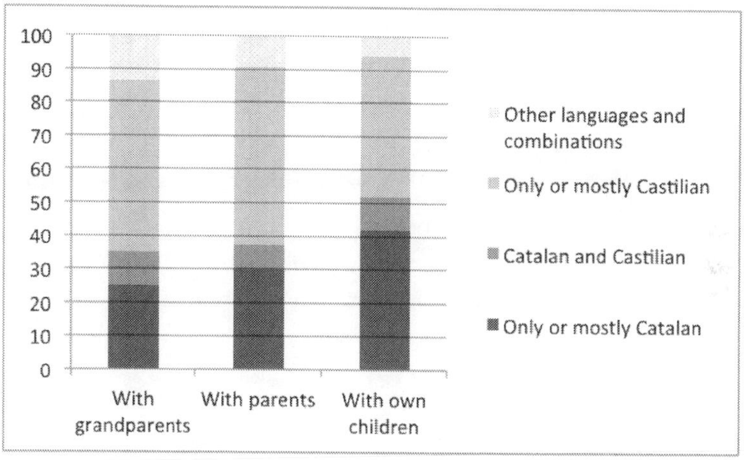

Source: Torres (2011: 85), out of EULP 2008

At any rate, Catalonia is one of Europe's most deeply bilingual societies, and the local language, in spite of a number of problems, faces no imminent demise. In fact, Catalan is a vibrant language that attracts new users. Half of the almost 5.7 million speakers of the language living in Catalonia proper did not learn the language from their parents, but rather from friends, at school, university, and so on.[1] The fact that 60 percent of all those born elsewhere in Spain and 42 percent of those born abroad declare that they too can speak Catalan bears testimony to the attraction of Catalan (EULP 2008). In fact, most of those who are more integrated use Catalan on an everyday basis, evidenced by the fact that one in every three people who spoke Castilian with their parents uses Catalan with their own offspring, basically in mixed couples (see Figure 1).

1 Source: Authors graphic created from EULP 2008 data and Sorolla (2011) Context demogràfic i econòmic. L'evolució de la comunitat lingüística. In: Pradilla, M.À. and Sorolla, N. (eds.) Informe sobre la situació de la llengua catalana (2008–2010). Barcelona: Observatori de la Llengua, pàg. 11. According to Sorolla (2011: 10), the total number of speakers of Catalan is 9.7 million.

The position of Catalan in Catalonia, a language without a state of its own, is unique in many respects. How has Catalan arrived at its current situation? To explain it, a bit of history is necessary. Especially in Europe, linguistically naive people tend to equate languages with sovereign states (e.g., France equals French), and therefore interpret discrepancies to this rule in terms of mixture. In their eyes, if Catalan is different from Spanish it *must* be a mixture between Spanish and, let's say, French and/or Italian. Simple as this rule may look, it is fundamentally wrong. Languages were there before any nation state was ever created. German, Italian or, in this case, Catalan, existed before Germany, Italy, or Spain were created. In fact, many states were created *on the basis* of a language, and not the other way around.

So what is Catalan, then? Catalan is the language that appeared in the territories we now call Catalonia in the early Middle Ages. As a language, it is derived from the Latin spoken in those territories 2,000 years ago, when the Roman Empire imposed it on the natives. In historical terms, then, Catalan is the indigenous language of Catalonia, and it has been used without interruption by virtually all the natives during most of the last millennium, in most social situations. Catalans have spoken Catalan at home and at work, in bars, in courts and in churches; they have sung songs, watched theatre, played sports, and written wills, laws, poetry, and novels in their language. In fact, until the 20th century, the vast majority of Catalans were *monolingual* Catalan speakers. So, in this crucial respect, the story of Catalan is not fundamentally different from that of many other "normal" languages in Europe.

But there is a fundamental difference between Catalan and other *normal* languages, and it has to do with its relationship with the State. Catalans started to write down their language more or less at the same time as the Portuguese, Italians, or Castilians. In fact, Catalan as a written language lived a golden age during the 14th and 15th centuries, when it was not only the main official and administrative language of a powerful state—the Crown of Aragon—but also as a literary and scientific language. But Catalan as a cultured language experienced two successive crises. The first one took place at the beginning of the 16th century, when the Crown of Aragon, Castile, Flanders, and Austria became united and formed the Habsburg Empire, the multinational, political entity that was the antecedent of Spain. When the imperial court moved to Castile, intellectuals and writers followed it, and Catalan literary production diminished abruptly in quantity and quality. The second crisis took place after Catalonia, Valencia, and the Balearic Islands were defeated during the War of Succession (1700–1714).Their territories were annexed to Castile, and their institutions were abolished—from courts and legal systems to universities—and replaced by Castilian ones. The new royal house started a policy of *castilianization* of Catalans which became a cornerstone of the new Spanish State. Following this policy, Catalan was progressively ousted from all formal positions, including the judiciary system, the administration, and the schools, with the declared goal of reducing it to the status of a spoken vernacular that could be eventually abandoned by its speakers. These goals were almost accomplished by General Franco's dictatorship (1936/39–1975), which banned Catalan from school and official spheres and spread knowledge of Castilian among all Catalans. Moreover, during this period, hundreds of thousands of Castilian-speaking immigrants settled in Catalonia, making Castilian a widely used language in Catalonia itself for the first time.

All in all, Catalan might have collapsed under such formidable pressures. But it didn't. Even during the darkest periods of repression, not only was the language spoken in everyday life by virtually all Catalans, but writers and intellectuals kept producing appreciable works with the hope that better times would eventually arrive. And they did after the dictator died.

Once democracy was established in Spain, Catalans managed to get some degree of autonomy in 1979 and started to reconstruct their society. A central element in this process was the *normalization* of the Catalan language. This process included two main activities. On the one hand, specific efforts had to be made to help the adult population—which had been deprived of a Catalan education—achieve language competence, which meant massive language literacy campaigns for almost all native speakers, and Catalan-as-a-second-language courses for Castilian-speaking immigrants. On the other hand, Catalan had to be (re)introduced in all those spheres of life from which it had been banned by the Spanish authorities. Catalan was therefore: (1) adopted again as the main language of administration in local and national institutions; (2) reinstated in schools and universities as the main language of instruction; (3) adopted as the vehicular language in a number of new mass-media; and (4) promoted in all spheres of life in general.

More than three decades after the dictator's death, the process has not been simple at all, and in several respects, it is still ongoing. Catalan is today a vibrant language, but it is not without major challenges. Let's summarize them in two parts: the societal and the political ones.

On the societal front, although Catalan has recovered significantly, it is still in many respects convalescing from three hundred years of repression.

For example, since 2011 virtually all newspapers edited in Catalonia appear either solely in Catalan or in two otherwise identical versions, one in Catalan and another one in Castilian. Local magazines are published mostly in Catalan. More than 10,000 different books are published every year in Catalan—including both local and international bestsellers—which is a greater number, for instance, than books published in Hebrew, Greek, or Finnish. But more newspapers and books are still sold in Castilian in Catalonia, not only because of monolingual immigrants, but also because even today, many adult locals feel more comfortable writing or reading in the language in which they were educated. The more than 1.5 million immigrants from all over the world who settled down in Catalonia in the first decade of the 2000s did not simplify the matter. The fact that Catalans readily switch to Castilian to speak to immigrants makes linguistic integration still more difficult.

Societal challenges are infinitely complicated due to the narrow margin of autonomy of Catalan institutions, and to the continuous political interference of the Spanish central authorities. At the end of the day, neither the Spanish State nor its Castilian national majority have ever accepted that Spain could become (again) a federal state where the different languages were dealt with on equal terms. On the contrary, during the last decades the central authorities have made every legal and political effort to ensure that Castilian always keeps an upper hand and all other languages are demoted. To offer one example, there are some areas outside of Catalonia proper, such as the *Franja*, where historically Catalan has been the dominant language but where it has received hardly any legal recognition at all. In Catalonia, the electoral system has made that degree of contempt impossible, but the efforts to keep Catalan in a secondary position have been constant. In this sense, the reaction to the 2006 new Statute of Autonomy is quite illustrative. After much controversy with the Spanish government, a Statute was passed in a referendum that made knowledge of Catalan mandatory for citizens of Catalonia, in order to put it on an equal footing with Castilian, which is mandatory for all Spanish citizens according to the 1978 Constitution. But in 2010, the Constitutional Court ruled that Castilian would be compulsory in Catalonia, but Catalan would not. And on the basis of this sentence, two years later the Spanish minister of education inflamed Catalonia when boasting in the parliament that it was his goal to *hispanicize* ("españolizar") Catalan students. He presented a bill that not only invaded Catalonia's jurisdiction in education, but allowed for Catalan children to be educated monolingually in Castilian, a position perceived as colonial and completely unacceptable to most Catalans.

In this context, are languages a major element for social mobilization in Catalonia right now? Yes and no. On the one hand, the defense of Catalan garners widespread cross-community support within Catalan society. One does not need to be a Catalan speaker to support the promotion of Catalan, among other things, because it is regarded as linguistic capital that plays an important role in the job market. Learning Catalan is a good investment in terms of social mobility, and promoting it is a good collective investment in terms of social cohesion and national identity. On the contrary, active mobilization in favor of Castilian, a global language that is known by everyone and which is imposed by the Spanish constitution, is more marginal. It is basically supported by a small, highly politicized—and usually Spanish immigrant—minority. It should not be forgotten that the leaders of the two major pro-independence parties have personally stated that in an independent Catalonia, Castilian would enjoy an official status. So, all in all, while languages are a fundamental element to understand Catalan society, they are not, at this moment, the pivotal element of the process of independence.

Catalonia, land of immigration

Andreu Domingo

Ph.D. in Sociology. Currently Deputy Director of the Centre for Demographics Studies (CED) at the Autonomous University of Barcelona (UAB), where he has been researcher since 1984. Main research areas are: demography, international migration, foreign population, marriage, family and kinship. He is the director of the Study Group for Demography and Migrations at the Centre for Demographic Studies.

Migrations and language: a system of social reproduction

In contrast with the rest of Spain, Catalonia has historically been a land of immigration. As of January 1, 2012, 18.6 percent of the 7.5 million inhabitants were born abroad, outside of Spain—mostly having arrived during the international migration boom at the beginning of the 21st century. Another 18 percent were born in other parts of Spain—products of the two waves of migration in the 20th century, and the remaining 63.4 percent were born in Catalonia. Close to 70 percent of the Catalan population is a direct or indirect result of contemporary migrations (that is, either an immigrant or a descendant of immigrants), and if we went back in time, this figure would cover an even larger majority of the population. Thus, like many other societies, including the United States itself, Catalan society faced what appears to be a worldwide tendency, accelerated by globalization. Its population growth, but also its economy, its society and culture, and in short, that which we call "identity" has largely been defined by the contributions of immigrants. Indeed, we can even consider immigration an endogenous factor of the population dynamic itself. It is precisely the increase in migratory movement that helped language—more than other differentiated characteristics of the Catalan culture—become the most defining, precisely because out of all the others—blood or ancestry, place of birth, religion, or race—it had the advantage of being the most inclusive.

In this way, and with the progressive arrival of migratory currents, the Catalan identity ended up defining itself as a reality of voluntary conscription, in which language serves as an anthropological marker. The use of Catalan or at least the respect for the Catalan language was the minimum act necessary for the integration process that, in exchange, promised upward social mobility, in other words, what all immigrant workers are after: the improvement of the living conditions in their own lives and those of their family. They end up defining membership with "A Catalan is whoever lives and works in Catalonia, and wants to be one." This may well be a Catalan version of the "American Dream"—with all of the extenuating circumstances that may need to be taken into account, and all of the disappointments obscured by a promise not always kept. The major difference, however, is not the volume of immigrant movement, but rather can be found in the lack of local institutions, and the subordinate role they play. The State not only has not respected the Catalan differences, but has openly persecuted them during the 40 years of the Francoist dictatorship between 1939–1976. During the so-called Democratic Transition the State put those differences in doubt at every opportunity (for example, with the coup d'état of 1981) and each time there has been a conservative majority in the Spanish Parliament. That explains why the bulk of integrating efforts has fallen almost exclusively to the citizenry. To make matters worse, the cyclical character of the migrations themselves, which follow the pattern of the general economic situation, made it so that in Catalonia, as in other countries of immigration, the moment when the maximum number of new residents arrived coincided with the turning point in the economic cycle, just as we are suffering currently.

An overview of migration in Catalonia during the 20th and 21st centuries

Apart from the massive population movements that took place in the formative period of Catalonia's history during the Middle Ages, due to the process of repopulating and colonizing the territories occupied by the kingdoms of Al Andalus, there is important historic evidence of significant migratory currents that originated in France during the 17th century and that also match the structure of modern Catalonia. Nonetheless, it wasn't until the last decades of the 19th century that Catalonia clearly became a society formed by immigration. The subsequent era was protagonized by migrations that came from the rest of Europe throughout the 20th century, divided into two great waves: the first at the beginning of the 20th century until the Spanish Civil War, and the second that began in the fifties, peaked in the sixties, and tapered off after the oil crisis of the mid 1970s. This second wave was followed by an international immigration boom which peaked in 2007 only to bottom out after the impact of the financial crisis since 2008 (See Graphic 1).

The first migratory wave which began in the first decade of the 20th century, benefited from the economic prosperity that came of Spain's neutrality during World War I, peaked at the end of the twenties, and then collapsed with the Crash of 1929 and fell definitively after the Spanish Civil War. These flows contributed to the growth of the population from the 1.9 million people at the beginning of the century to 2.7 million in 1930. The second wave is responsible for an influx of 350,574 people between 1961–1966. This second 20th-century migration blended into the economic crisis of the second half of the seventies, which ended up resulting in a net negative migration of 85,443 people less between 1981–1985. The virtual stagnation of the population at 6 million for more than 20 years is seen until the second half of the nineties. In this way, the total growth between 1951–1976 was 2.4 million people, which almost doubled the population of 3.2 million people in 1950 to the 5.7 million who were registered in 1975. Immigration was responsible for 57.8 percent of this growth. These rates were comparable to immigrant attractor countries like Argentina or the United States, and reveal how Catalonia maintained its proportion in relative terms with respect to the worldwide population, which was undergoing a population explosion. The international character of the migratory currents intensified in both volume and proportion of immigrants. That is how a population increase of 83,804 in 1991–1995 turned into 132,819 in 1991–1996, and reached a new record in the first five years of the new millennium with 722,753 new immigrants. The population thus grew from 6 million to 7.5 million in little less than a decade, a factor of 1.2 thanks, as we've seen, fundamentally to immigration, and in a much smaller measure, to the increase in birth rate that the immigrants themselves contributed. Nevertheless, migration made up a whopping 91 percent of this growth.

Graphic 1: Migratory growth, five-year natural growth, and evolution of the population in Catalonia from 1901 to 2010.

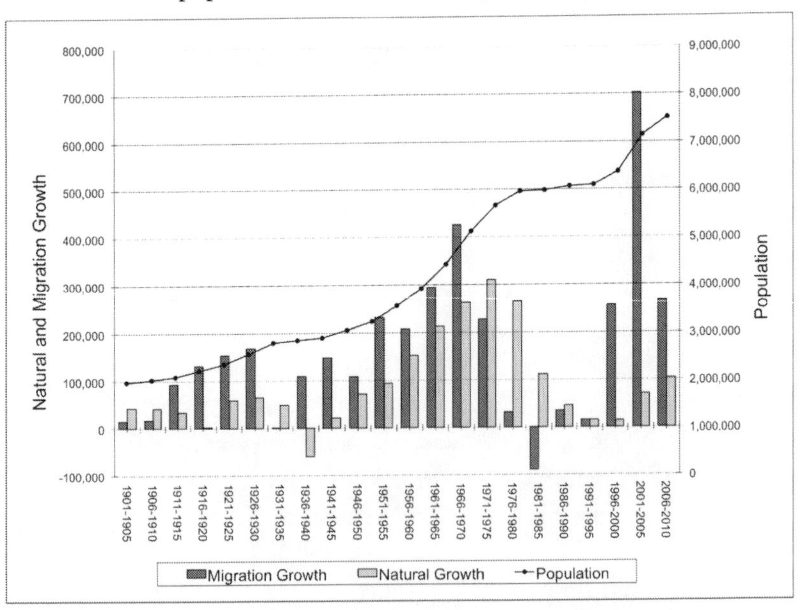

Source: Created by the author from Census and Registration records of the Padró Continu (INE).

Spanish nationalism on the attack

The Spanish conservative government has gone on a two-pronged offensive against the political autonomy of Catalonia: first by provoking discord among those who live in Catalonia by calling language use into question and second by making it difficult for immigrants to integrate themselves into the community. It's for that reason that the principal attacks, beginning with the economic plundering, have been directed at the education system, and in particular the Catalan linguistic immersion system that has been in place since 1983 and the Law of Immigrant Integration approved by the Catalan Parliament in 2010. On the one hand, they're looking to substitute history subject matter with standardized texts that impose the story of Spanish nationalism—in which Spain's origins are confused with the origins of time and racial unity—and at the same time relegate education of the Catalan language to a second tier, in the name of the international power of the Spanish language, or as they like to remind us, the "language of the 300 million". Spanish nationalism is dressed up in progressivism, liberalism, cosmopolitanism, and internationalism in order to achieve the recognition of a binational character of Catalonia, and thus to create a "Spanish-speaking linguistic community" as a splintered political entity within the Catalan reality, and depends directly on an ethnic rereading of the demographic history of Catalonia.

It's telling that empirical data—almost 70 percent of the Catalan population is a direct or indirect result 20th and 21st-century immigration—is constantly repeated by Spanish nationalists to defend the assertion that only a third of the population in Catalonia is Catalan. This affirmation presupposes that Catalan identity is only defined through blood, and what is more, that any contamination with foreign blood is discarded from this ethnic calculation. This interpretation clearly contradicts what has been the definition of Catalan identity that has been forged throughout the 20th century, a definition that has tried, more or less successfully to translate the demographic reality, to wit: that the demographic reproduction (and the social reproduction) of Catalonia includes immigration as an endogenous factor, since it is as important as biological reproduction and often contributes even more than the birth rate to Catalonia's population growth. In a way, that they use the data in this way shouldn't surprise us, since the obsession of pure blood (and religion) has been an essential component of Spanish nationalism. They are projecting in Catalonia their historic patterns of exclusion and homogenization. From this desire, whose objective is none other than to downplay Catalan identity in Catalonia, the revisionist reading in the demographic field is accompanied by negationism in the historic field. According to the latter, the Catalan language has never been persecuted, the Francoist repression has never existed, and the Decrees of *Nova Planta*—with which the self-governing institutions of Catalonia were completely erased and the Catalan language was banished and replaced by Spanish after the defeat of September 11, 1714—was just a way of modernizing the country (Spain).

Opening the black box of secessionism

Laia Balcells

Assistant professor of political science at Duke University and affiliated researcher at the Institute for Economic Analysis, CSIC (Barcelona). Balcells teaches and does research on topics of political violence, nationalism and ethnic conflict, and fiscal federalism.

For a long time, social scientists have studied nationalism and ethnic conflict from multiple dimensions. They have analyzed how ethnic diversity affects governance in democratic countries, trust and reciprocity, violent conflict, civil wars, and resistance to foreign occupation, among other things. The results tend to be pessimistic, although there are some optimistic findings such as that ethnic heterogeneity is not significantly related to violent conflict[1] or that altruism is not intrinsically related to coethnicity.[2] In comparative politics, secessionism has often been connected to the study of ethnic politics and ethnic conflict; secession and partition have been analyzed as possible solutions to civil war, with some positive answers,[3] but also some negative ones.[4] In political theory, on the other hand, the focus has been on the normative exploration of the "right to secede". One of the most influential theorists of secession, Allen Buchanan, has argued that the right to secede is related to Locke's "right to revolution".[5] In other words, it is a remedial right that should be conceded only when there have been major injustices suffered by those demanding it. Buchanan also reflects on the fact that a credible threat to exit can generate a *de facto* "minority veto". For example, Catalonia could threaten Spain with secession every time there was a disagreement with policies enacted from Madrid. Even though Buchanan recognizes that the principle of territorial integrity of the states reduces the bargaining potential of "the threat to exit" (by a minority), he does not elaborate much on the reverse of this argument, which is the following: a credible threat not to allow exit (by the state) can generate a *de facto* minority veto within the territory claiming secession. For example, the Spanish government led by the *Partido Popular*—a political party that controls a majority in Spain's central

---

1 Fearon, James, and David Laitin. 2003. "Ethnicity, Insurgency, and Civil War" *American Political Science Review* 97 (1): 75–86.

2 Habyarimana, J, M. Humphreys, D. Posner and J. Weinstein. 2009 *Coethnicity: Diversity and the Dilemmas of Collective Action*. New York: Russell Sage Press.

3 Kaufman, Chaim. 1998. "When All Else Fails. Ethnic Population Transfers and Partitions in the Twentieth Century" *International Security* 23(2): 120–156; Downes, Alexander. "The Holy Land Divided: Defending Partition as a Solution to Ethnic Wars" *Security Studies* 10/4 (Summer 2001): 58–116.

4 Sambanis, Nicholas. 2000. "Partition as a Solution to Ethnic War: An Empirical Critique of the Theoretical Literature." *World Politics* 52: 437–83. Sambanis, Nicholas and Jonah Schulhofer-Wohl. 2009. "What's In A Line? Is Partition the Solution to Civil War?" *International Security* 34 (2): 82–118.

5 Buchanan, Allen. 1997. "Theories of Secession" *Philosophy & Public Affairs* 26(1): 36–61.

government (and many other autonomous communities and municipalities in Spain) and yet is a minority party in Catalonia—can undertake policies that endanger the economic and cultural survival of Catalonia because the government knows that the exit of Catalonia from Spain is not legally feasible in the current constitutional framework, and that this framework is extremely difficult to change. The question is whether, following Buchanan's theory, these policies can be considered unjust enough to legitimize the right of secession. In other words, we can wonder about the exact limits beyond which injustices make secession legitimate. According to Catalan nationalists, these limits were surpassed long ago in Catalonia, those against secession nonetheless challenge this notion.

The study of secession is still quite minimal in social sciences and, when it takes place, the discussion is somewhat contaminated by what can be called an "anti-secessionist bias". Indeed, secession is often conceived as the last of the remedies (e.g., in Sudan), as a possible source of new conflicts (e.g., in the Balkans), or as a disastrous solution to intractable conflicts (e.g., in Iraq). There is little research that takes secessionism as a neutral phenomenon and studies its causes and consequences freed from normative considerations.[6]

The origins of this bias are manifold. First, there is the influence of the United States in academia. The United States was marked by a secessionist civil war in its origins as a state, and secessionism was, in that case, related to the willingness to preserve an unfair *status quo* (that is, slavery). So people tend to associate secessionism with conservatism. Second, there is the neoliberal influence on the idea that competition among governance units has a positive influence on achieving optimal tax rates. This engenders suspicion of secession among leftist spheres, especially when such demands occur in relatively wealthy territories such as Catalonia or Flanders, and it is conceived as a movement led by selfish, ethnic entrepreneurs and/or territories. Yet, the existence of social-democratic and extreme-left factions in contemporary secessionist movements or the existence of secessionism in relatively poor regions such as Corsica or Québec constitute solid evidence against the hypothesis that secessionism is motivated only out of selfish motives (that is, an unwillingness to redistribute). Finally, secessionism has been perceived as the main cause of violent conflict in the world. The correlation between secessionism and civil war is high: 46 percent of all civil wars taking place

---

6 An example of non-normative type of work on this topic is: Sambanis, Nicholas and Branko Milanovic. 2011. Explaining the demand for sovereignty. The World Bank. Development Research Group.

between 1944 and 2004 involve a secessionist movement.[7] Nonetheless, the mechanisms underlying this relationship are not clear. On the one hand, self-determination movements get involved in violent conflict very often as a *response* to repressive actions perpetrated by the states.[8] On the other hand, lack of access to power by ethnic minorities (and not secessionism *per se*) often explains the onset of violent conflict.[9]

It is extremely important to establish regularities and to study secessionism analytically. Yet, this phenomenon should not be conceived monolithically. I would argue that, in the same way that scholars have identified different types of nationalism,[10] we should be able to identify different types of secessionism. It is almost unnecessary to say that the current secessionist movement in Texas has little in common with the one in Québec, for example. Also, there may be important differences among the groups that constitute a secessionist movement. For example, in the case of Catalonia, the secessionism represented by the liberal political party Convergència i Unió (CiU) cannot be equated to that of the extreme left-wing coalition Coalició d'Unitat Popular (CUP), whose members self-identify as a "liberation movement".[11]

Finally, we need to be aware of the anti-secessionist bias in mass media, and not just in academic research. It has been only recently that important newspapers and magazines have started to take secessionist movements

---

7 Balcells, Laia and Stathis Kalyvas. 2012. The Marxist Paradox. National liberation versus ethnic insurgencies. Unpublished Manuscript, Duke University and Yale University.

8 Sambanis, Nicholas and Annalisa Zinn. 2005. "From Protest to Violence: An Analysis of Conflict Escalation with an Application to Self-Determination Movements" (Unpublished Manuscript). Paper presented at the annual meeting of the American Political Science Association, Marriott Wardman Park, Omni Shoreham, Washington Hilton, Washington, DC.

9 Cederman, Lars-Erik, Kristian Skrede Gleditsch, and Nils B. Weidmann. 2011. "Horizontal Inequalities and Ethnonationalist Civil War: A Global Comparison." American Political Science Review 105 (3): 478–495.

10 As Hechter has explained, patriotism cannot be equated to peripheral nationalism. He also distinguishes irrendentism, state building nationalism, and unification nationalism. (Hechter, Michael. 2000. *Containing Nationalism*. Oxford and New York: Oxford University Press.)

11 Catalan secessionism is a complex phenomenon with much internal fractionalization and heterogeneity. As Hilari Raguer explains, there are two main branches of Catalan nationalism: one that is Catholic and right wing, and one that is republican and left wing. But they both share common ground, which is Catalan secessionism's civic character and its pacifist nature.

such as the ones going in Catalonia and Scotland *(e.g. the Guardian, the New York Times, the Huffington Post, Reuters)* seriously. But other media outlets are highly skeptical of these movements and therefore indirectly or directly supportive of the status quo of the existing national states. Nonetheless, journalists are likely to become less biased towards this issue once academics become less so, and once the reality of the facts such as those taking place in Catalonia, Flanders, and Scotland shows that secessionism is not necessarily connected to disastrous events. Indeed, in all of these cases, secessionism is civic, democratic, and pacific, and highly unlikely to escalate into an armed conflict anytime in the future.

In a nutshell, I would argue that it is important to approach the issue of secessionism with an analytical lens, and to do so by exploring all of its complexity. By opening the black box of secessionism, the so-called anti-secessionist bias should be dismantled. This should allow us not only to provide better explanations for this phenomenon but also for more appropriate policy recommendations regarding these movements and the states that are confronting them.

Schooling in Catalonia (1978–2012)

Pere Mayans Balcells

Professor of Secondary Catalan Language and Literature Education. Mayans was previously director of the Catalan Teaching Service and the Service of Immersion and Language Use and currently is director of the Language Immersion and Welcome Service (all of which are part of the Education Department of the Catalan Government). These departments are responsible for linguistic immersion, education in Catalan, welcoming newly arrived students, managing languages in educational centers, promoting Catalan literature, and so forth. Author of several books and more than 200 articles on sociolinguistic reality of the Catalan Countries and of other minority languages in the world.

Catalonia has been, without a doubt, the part of the Catalan Countries in which the political and social consensus have had the broad support necessary to make Catalan the principal language of the educational system—even more so than in Andorra, currently the only independent state where Catalan is spoken.

It must be pointed out that the model came out of democratic decision making. Right from the start, the Catalan Statute of Autonomy of 1979 established Catalan as its own official language (though sharing official status with Spanish). In order to level out the situation of the two official languages, and keeping in mind the situation of the Catalan language, which at all levels is clearly and indisputably inferior to that of Spanish (indeed, it's appropriate to use the word "precarious", the term that appears in the preamble of Law 7/1983 of April 18, for linguistic normalization in Catalonia), Catalan was made the primary language of certain public arenas. These arenas include toponomy, Catalonia's local government offices, public (Catalan) media outlets, and nonuniversity education. Keep in mind that the Linguistic Normalization Law was approved by a vote of 132 votes in favor, out of a total of 135.

In this article, we'll focus on reviewing the process that was followed in order to make Catalan the language of instruction in Catalonia[1] and which can be divided into five principal stages (the fifth of which is just beginning).

1. Establishing a model for Catalan in Education (1978–1983), right in the midst of the democratic political transition of the Spanish State after the death of the dictator Francisco Franco. The newly created Catalan Autonomous Administration was able to make Catalan a required subject, with three hours of classroom instruction per week. By 1983, 90 percent of the student

---

1 Unfortunately, the process has not been the same throughout the rest of the Catalan territories. In Franja de Ponent, a Catalan-speaking territory within the Autonomous Community of Aragon, Catalan as an elective has been chosen by 81.76 percent of the student body (4,693 students compared with 791 during the 1984–1985 school year or 3,045 in the 1994–1995 school year). In addition, some Catalan/Spanish bilingual courses have been added to the curriculum. (In addition to being taught as a language, Catalan has also been used as the language of instruction for some courses.) In Valencian Country, Catalan curricula have gradually increased to about 30 percent of the student body (2009–2010), but at any rate, have not kept up with demand in the slightest. In the Balearic and Pitiusic Islands, the advance of Catalan has been significant: 50 percent of the non-university educational centers use Catalan as the language of instruction (with Spanish as a subject) while the other 50 percent use both languages to varying degrees.

population in nursery school through primary school had studied Catalan in school.

2. The progressive establishment of instruction in Catalan. This period began with the already mentioned Law of Linguistic Normalization of 1983, which roughly dictated that Catalan would be the principal language used in primary and secondary education. It also recognized the right of children to receive their first schooling in their primary language, either Catalan or Spanish, required that both Catalan and Spanish languages be taught at all levels of non-university education, kept students of different language backgrounds together, and guaranteed that all schoolchildren in Catalonia, no matter what language they used when they began school, could correctly and normally use both Catalan and Spanish at the end of their basic studies.

The success of this educational initiative was indisputable, and it benefited from the support of practically all of the members of the Parliament of Catalonia. It was clear that even heavily Spanish-speaking areas (with 70 percent of Spanish speakers) took advantage of, with little resistance, the Program of Linguistic Immersion, that guaranteed the use of Catalan as the language of instruction, especially in the early school years. According to data from the Department of Education, in the 1992–1993 school year, Catalan was the language of instruction of 63 percent of the nursery schools and primary schools in Catalonia.

It's important to point out the task of updating the tens of thousands of teachers and professors across Catalonia—more than 50,000—was huge and received support from both Catalan universities as well as the teacher unions.

3. Extending the Catalan model. At the beginning of the 1992–1993 school year, the curricula generated from the State's Organic Law of the Education System (1990) were approved, which in Catalonia were laid out via decrees that establish the hierarchy of nonuniversity education. It was declared that Catalan would be used both as the language of instruction and as an independent subject at all levels. In this way, a single school model was decided on. Nevertheless, two principles from the earlier era still applied: the right to choose Spanish as the language of instruction for the very first years (which fewer and fewer families took advantage of) and the objective that the students acquire the same proficiency in both official languages by the end of their compulsory education. This is the era in which Catalan is consolidated as the most often used language in the education system.

4. The wave of migration from all over the world to Catalonia at the beginning of the 21st century—the numbers went from 24,787 students from foreign countries in the 2000–2001 school year to 155,845 students in the 2009–2010 school year—shook up the linguistic model of Catalan schooling, which had convinced itself of the strength of Catalan despite the important gaps that still remained. These gaps continue, with respect to teaching foreign languages, the language level of the teachers themselves, and in some places, the fact that some teachers continued—and continue—to give class in Spanish.

The response from the Catalan administration with respect to the new immigration was to create specific programs in Catalan to serve these students. (Had they not made this effort, the new students would probably have ended up in an overwhelming number of Spanish-speaking classrooms throughout the country.) The development of School Adaptation Workshops and the Plan for Language and Social Cohesion with the creation of 1,000 "welcome" classrooms were principal components of these programs. The new reality throughout the country in 2007 pushed the Ministry of Education, at that point headed by the Socialist Ernest Maragall, to begin an Updated Plan of the Linguistic Immersion Program, which responded to the new sociolinguistic reality of the country, both in primary and secondary education.

In addition, during this period, serious proposals were made more or less throughout the system to add curriculum content in English or French, both in primary and secondary education, using systems that integrate language and content instruction.

5. In 2010, the Spanish Constitutional Court ruled against the Statute of Autonomy and, in particular, against the fact that Catalan is the only language of instruction in Catalonia's education system. The court said that in cases where Catalan is considered to be normalized, instruction should tend toward an equal percentage of classes in both official languages. Clearly, the rulings that are derived from this one seem to be opening a new legal framework for the presence of Catalan in our educational system. Of course, we would much rather close this period saying that we have gotten through this legal impasse, and that in the end Catalonia's schools will continue to be democratically decided on from the Parliament of Catalonia, but the attacks from the Spanish government continue. Recently (December 2012), the Spanish Minister of Education (José Ignacio Wert), went too far. In the proposed

Organic Law for the Improvement of the Quality of Education, several suggestions were made that directly undermine the position of Catalan in the educational system:

a. The school councils will guarantee in all of the required educational levels that the co-official languages shall be offered in the various subjects in balanced proportions with respect to hours of class time, in order to ensure proficiency in both languages by the students, without inhibiting the possibility of including foreign languages.

b. It is the responsibility of the school councils to determine the proper proportion necessary of the use of Spanish and the co-official language as languages of instruction in the educational system, according to the current state of linguistic normalization.

c. The school councils can approve, in function of the state of linguistic normalization within their territories, special treatment for the co-official language with respect to Spanish in a reasonable proportion, as long as Spanish is not excluded.

d. While the determination referred to in the previous paragraph has not been made, the parents or guardians will have the right to choose the language of instruction that their children will receive. When, as a result of the determination not being made, there is no public or semi-public school in the chosen language of instruction in the city or town in which the students reside, the parents or guardians may choose to send their children to private schools, and the administration will have to underwrite the cost.

First of all, students are required to be proficient in the State language by the time they leave elementary school. This is already guaranteed by Catalonia's education system, and is stipulated in our curricula and is demonstrated by the statewide (and Catalonia-wide) Spanish linguistic competency tests that are administered. So far, so good. The problem arises from the requirement that the languages of instruction be offered in "equal proportions" (they don't talk about language instruction, but rather languages of instruction). At any rate, they allow the autonomous communities to determine the final division according to the state of "linguistic normalization" (a term that, as everyone knows, is relative, because what does linguistic normalization really mean anyway?), which would allow a "differentiated" treatment of the co-official, e.g., non-Spanish, language to a "reasonable degree" (again, a term of calculated ambiguity), without that meaning that Spanish should not be the language of instruction.

As you can see, the perspective is quite far from the spirit of the Catalan rules, which since 1983, were established as we've seen, so that Catalan as a language of instruction could compensate the sociolinguistic reality of the two official languages in Catalonia and guarantee, therefore, the right of all citizens to know them (something that is not guaranteed, for example, by the educational system in the Valencian Country, where children who are schooled in Catalan end up knowing both Catalan and Spanish, while children who are taught in Spanish mostly are not competent in our language, which is only taught as an additional subject). It's clear that the model proposed by the Minister puts into question not only Catalan education but the application of the very methodologies of linguistic immersion.

To hammer it home, however, he threatens (no other term is more accurate) that while the educational administration in charge does not establish these percentages, the parents or guardians have the right to choose the language of instruction for the schooling of their children. What is more, if such options don't exist in their school, the parents or guardians can choose to send their children to private schools, whose costs must be taken care of by the corresponding local school administration. Indeed, these statements make us consider various questions: in Catalonia do schools even exist that use Spanish exclusively as the language of instruction? In the Valencian Country, will parents who ask for schooling in Valencian also have this same right (or will the trilingualism decree that already establishes the percentages make it a moot point?) Can private schools really be funded with public monies?

With respect to the ranking of languages that this bill proposes, Catalan (and the other co-official languages of the State) are relegated to a third category of subjects. There are the "principal" ones (Spanish, and the first foreign language), the "specifics" (which include the second foreign language), and then finally, the "specialties", which could include a co-official language. In this draft, in addition, it is noted that Catalan material (or any other co-official language's material) would not be used for individual evaluation to determine the level of competency. It seems, however, that faced with the reactions against this bill, that the minister has retracted this clear discrimination. The same goes for the final evaluations for secondary school.

It's remarkable that the entire offensive against Catalan being the primary language in Catalonia's schools is carried out despite official reports—such as the General Diagnostic Evaluation 2010, published by the Spanish Ministry of Education—demonstrating that the Catalan schoolchildren's linguistic competency in Spanish is on a par with the average across the Spanish State, and indeed, is superior to that of some monolingual communities like the Canary Islands, Extremadura, or Andalusia, or of bilingual communities where Spanish has a much stronger presence as a language of instruction (as in the Balearic Islands, Galicia, and the Valencian Country).

Finally, it's essential to point out that the current educational system in Catalonia has guaranteed equal opportunity (that is, linguistic opportunity) to all of the citizens of Catalonia that have passed through our compulsory education system in the last few decades. Everyone who has been schooled is able to understand, write, read, and speak both Catalan and Spanish, regardless of their family language situation. That is why this model has been praised by the High Level Group on Multilingualism, created by the European Commission in 2005, regardless of how little that seems to matter to the Spanish government.

The view from Brussels

Ramon Tremosa i Balcells

Member of the European Parliament since 2009. Economic & Finance and Transports Committees. EP Rapporteur on new European financial supervision (2010), ECB Report (2011) and Competition Report (2012). Deputy speaker for the liberal-democrat group in the directives "European Single Railway Area" and "Airport Package". Follows debates on Mediterranean Rail Corridor and ACP reform. Professor of Economic Theory at University of Barcelona (1992–2009). Author of several articles and books on monetary policy, regional economics, and fiscal federalism, including Catalonia, An Emerging Economy *(Sussex Academic Press, 2010) and* L'espoli fiscal [Fiscal Plunder] *(2004).*

1. Catalonia is seen by the EU as the most Scandinavian country in the Mediterranean: an industrial, exporting, creative country (28 percent of Spanish exports in 2011), with a city like Barcelona, willing and able to be a great European capital, and an intercontinental commercial seaport. Catalonia indeed is seen by the EU as a model for Mediterranean countries, thanks to the 4,000 multinational companies installed in its territory and its powerful system of Research and Development. (Catalonia is one of the top regions to receive R&D funds from the EU.)

After all, Europe and Germany want countries that work, whose governments pay their bills after 30 days, where the labor markets are efficient, the judicial system is swift, the legal security of international investments is effectively protected, and where infrastructures earn money because they are located where they help grow the economy instead of losing money hand over fist because they're built where there is nothing and nobody. In other words, everything that Spain currently does not offer. "Spain has failed once again," I often hear in the EU. "Spain has lost the economic war against itself," as former Catalan President Pujol said. If an independent Catalonia guarantees the opposite of what is currently offered by Spain, Europe's doors will be wide open to it.

How have Catalans gotten to this point? The answer is easy enough to give, now that the international press is discovering the territorial aspects of Spain's ruinous economic regional model that the PP and PSOE have imposed during approximately the past 30 years (it was they who invented the 17 autonomous communities). This Spanish model is now revealed to have an absolutely radial, centralist system of infrastructures and an obsessive monopolization of all of the spheres of power (tax collection, airports, trains, ports, judicial system, and so on), powers that in federal systems are shared between the central government and the regional ones. If we add to that the ongoing, constant inefficiencies of a lazy Spanish State insensitive to the changes in globalization (late payments from the central government; dual, inefficient labor market; insecure legal status of international investments; slow judicial system; obsessive bureaucracy; compulsive overregulation; arbitrary and confiscatory fiscal inspections; disastrous energy policy (bungling electricity tariffs, for example), the Catalan answer to the European question is obvious. And if we add to that the prohibitions on speaking Catalan, in force to this day in the European Parliament, and the nonstatewide co-officialty of Catalan in contrast with the situation in Finland, Belgium, or

Switzerland, the growing Catalan demands for having their own state become more and more understandable.

2. No territory belonging to a member state of the EU has ever seceded before, and therefore, there is no precedent that can serve as a model. Now, the fact that the EU and the European Commission are preparing for this eventuality is an open secret, given that the Scottish Referendum of 2014 is on the horizon, possibly in October. If that happens, we will have to proceed toward internal enlargement of the EU and Scotland will ask for the automatic subrogation of all of the treaties in force to which it is a party thanks to Great Britain, setting aside other matters like whether or not to join the Euro.

At any rate, it will be in the interest of the EU and the ECB and all the other European organizations to have the process of internal enlargement proceed as quickly as possible, in order to reduce to a minimum the uncertainties and costs that a significant institutional process of change, such as creating a new state, will generate. If there is clear political will, the precedent of the rapid reunification of Germany is what we must invoke. That event was also not foreseen in any treaty, but, at the moment of truth, freedom and democracy trumped legal documents. Europe and the EU are still a house in which the values of freedom and democracy are fundamental and override any legal documents currently in force.

In Great Britain, no constitution is necessary for the Scots to have the freedom to decide their own future, if they so decide. In Spain, the Constitution of 1978 is interpreted in a fundamentalist, radical, immutable fashion and is used against the growing desires for freedom from increasing numbers of Catalans.

3. Last October, the British Parliament published a report on its website about how Scotland might end up in the EU after a hypothetical victory of the "yes" vote in the 2014 referendum. The report was written by the prestigious Oxford Professor Graham Avery, Honorary General Director of the European Commission.

With respect to how the Scottish State would be integrated into the EU, Avery said that if the Scots have been citizens of the EU for forty years, and they want to continue to be so, then it would be difficult to make them leave and reenter. "Scotland is not Turkey," he said, and the Scots can't be treated as if they were citizens of a country that has never formed part of the EU, as in the case of the Turks. Graham Avery said that the most logical solution would be to put Scotland on a "fast-track" like the ones they have in airports for frequent travelers.

This opinion was initially defended by the Spanish Commissioner himself, Joaquín Almunia, who in October 2012 said in Barcelona that it is not clear that European citizens with acquired rights (and the currency, as in the case of the Catalans) could be so easily disenfranchised from one day to the next, in the case of secession of a territory of a state that is already a member of the EU.

In the midst of the campaign of fear and threats launched by the PP and PSOE against a case of hypothetical independence, incapable as they are of offering anything positive to Catalans (such as the "better together" campaign that the English offer the Scots), on last November 3, *The Economist* published a very interesting article. In the most influential economic weekly magazine in the world, it said that "a Spain that is ultra-dependent on the EU with respect to rescues and interventions cannot veto the incorporation of an independent Scotland into the EU." This opinion roundly contradicts Spanish Minister of Foreign Affairs García-Margallo's repeated statements that any new country will "have to get in line" behind the current candidates.

4. On May 16, 2012 in the *Financial Times*, David Gardner wrote an article titled "Spain: devolution can be a part of the solution" in which he backed the extension of the Basque economic agreement to Catalonia as one of the possible solutions to the current Spanish crisis (both economic and institutional), while alleging motives of economic efficiency and better tax collection management. In Europe, the countries that have experienced a quick economic recovery at the end of 2009 until the middle of 2011—thanks to a brilliant recovery of industrial exports and the previous restoration of bank credit flow to businesses and families—have been the small central European, Scandinavian, and Baltic states.

The midsize and larger states in the South of Europe (those known as PIIGS, France, and the UK), in contrast, are those that have shown less recovery and a larger recurrence or that have spent the last five years in free fall, as in the case of Spain. Germany is the exception that proves the rule: while it is the largest country in the European Union in terms of population and GDP, its success is attributed to the true fiscal federalism that the Allies imposed after the Second World War, inspired by the federalist system in place in the United States. Germany, in fact, works well thanks to the fact that it acts like

17 independent Denmarks. Its 17 *länder* or federal states have a taxation agency that collects all of the major taxes, and with the money in their own pocket, they negotiate equalizing transfers between regions and thus limit transfers to Berlin. (The principle of ordinality limits de facto the transfers to 3–4 percent of regional GDP in the net contributing states. A net contributing state cannot, after distribution, be below the per capita income of a net receiving state.) This true fiscal federalism, very similar to that of the three Basque regions and that of Navarre, doesn't damage the unity of the market because of this truly federal fact: real federalism according to the academic definition is that in which the regions collect the major taxes, and not just spend them as in Spain.

In the same way, the 17 German *länder* have sovereign powers over providing for and managing their infrastructure, like being able to decide whether to construct airports or the concessions of airline slots in function of their specific economic interests (financial, export, touristic) of each state or *länd*. I have heard the president of Deutsche Bahn, Dr. Rudiger Grübe, the largest German (and European) train company explain how he has to renegotiate 17 regional management contracts each year, while competing with the 300 train operators in Germany.

"Economic integration and political disintegration" is a key article published in 2000 in *American Economic Review* by the MIT professors Alessina and Spolaore, who expanded the article into their now classic book *The Size of Nations* in 2003. The more open and interdependent the world becomes, the more the incentives grow for small countries to choose to create their own efficient, more homogeneous, and governable states, because of the efficient management of their inhabitants' preferences (wide consensus is easier to achieve, there is more flexibility in productive markets . . .). Catalonia, at this decisive moment in which it is carefully reevaluating the newly failed Madridian centralism, is paying attention. In fact, everything that works right now in Catalonia is tied to the Europe of small efficient states, while that which is not working is still tied to constant, decadent centralism.

5. Multinational companies and independence: the great Catalan economist Miquel Puig maintains, in a very interesting series of articles in the daily *Ara*, that "the debate about the independence of Catalonia is much more sentimental than it is rational". The 4,000 multinational companies in Catalonia today know very well that if they were in a normal country (with a Mediterranean rail corridor, local efficient management of ports, airports, and trains, timely payment of bills, efficient labor and energy markets, legal stability of investments, and so on) their sales and earnings would multiply. These 4,000 companies, the day after the Catalan Parliament votes in favor of a sovereign state, will continue to send their trucks, ships, and trains back and forth as if nothing has changed. "There is nothing rational to argue about on this point," concludes Miquel Puig.

Seen from Brussels, it's important to note that Madrid's threats of expulsion from the euro and from the EU if Catalonia unilaterally proclaims its independence are not very credible. If there is any country that runs the risk of being forced out of the euro it is the centralist, Jacobin, inefficient Spain that is incapable of shucking its secular isolationism and adapting itself to an open and globalized world like the one we live in in the 21st century. If Catalonia were thrown out of the euro, the 4,000 multinational companies in Catalonia would remain out of self-interest and they might even be able to influence the quick interior amplification that is already being considered and studied by the EU in the case that Scotland ends up voting in favor of its independence.

It is curious that the country that threatens vetoes and expulsions from the EU be Spain, a country whose ruinous economy and incapacity to reform itself by imitating good European practices, is putting at risk not only the common currency but even the whole European project itself. We have to remember that more than the EU itself (an embryo of political union that still has no fiscal power, no bank unity, and not enough democratic legitimacy) is the European economic space in which people, products, and capital can circulate freely. Norway and Switzerland are not part of the EU but they insist on access to this free circulation because it is the most successful European invention of the last 60 years. And they are the two most prosperous countries in the world according to many economic and social indexes.

Therefore, the British movement to leave the EU (but not this European economic space that they call the *internal market*) might indicate that they foresee the failure of the process in which the EU finds itself at this historic crossroads: or more union (fiscal, banking, political . . .) or renationalization. What most certainly has no future is a union in which the most efficient labor market in the world (Denmark) lives together with the most inefficient labor market in the world (Spain). Economic divergence is guaranteed.

As one of the English governors of Menorca said in the 18th century, "the Castilians are arrogant, intolerant, and what is worse, they don't have a single good idea." It would be nice if this sentiment were untrue and that we Catalans could vote freely and without threats on what we think is best. Today Europe is still a place where freedom and democracy are the pillars and the fundamental values of political action, as demonstrated by David Cameron giving the Scots a referendum that he does not want, but that the Scots do. Because as MEP Daniel Cohn-Bendit, no friend of nationalisms has said, "if the process is transparent, peaceful, democratic, and wins a majority, the EU will end up accepting an independent Catalonia."

Keep Calm and Speak Catalan

Josep Maria Ganyet

Degree in Computer Engineering from the Autonomous University of Barcelona, specializing in Artificial Intelligence. Ganyet has worked in Human Computer Interaction, design, teaching, and communication at IBM, Deutsche Bank, and Gotomedia. He has also created several online communication and web design startups as well as one focused on archaeology. He wrote a pioneering blog in 1998 in which he narrated the adventures of a medieval knight in the United States (in Old Catalan). Currently, he directs the design studio Mortensen.co, is part of a startup, gives classes at the Universitat Pompeu Fabra, contributes to RAC1 radio, and is working on a book. He writes at Ganyet.com and speaks six languages.

"We don't inherit language from our ancestors,
we borrow it from our children."
Loose adaption of a Native American proverb

A tweet from 2012

On December 4, 2012, I was riding the train to work listening to the radio and following my Twitter stream, as I'm wont to do. The topic of the day was the education reform bill with which the Spanish education minister was attempting to change the current unified Catalan school system into one in which children are to be segregated by language—Catalan or Spanish—according to the parents' preferences.

While the radio chat show guests criticized and debated the topic with more or less vehemence, my Twitter timeline bubbled over with a mixed bag of indignant, funny, and viscerally angry tweets.

And it was while reading the multiple and irate reactions on Twitter that the phrase "Keep Calm and Carry On" popped into my head. I adapted it to "Keep Calm and Speak Catalan" (in English) and sent it on its Twitter way. It was a declaration of principles, mixed with irony, history, and future that could be interpreted as: we'll just keep doing what we're doing as if nothing happened.

A tweet from 1939

I have to confess that even though I had read about the original Keep Calm and Carry On and even though I had seen the original version (and many of the thousand and one adaptations that have been made since, some more successful than others) I wasn't aware of the exact context, the history, or the mystique behind the poster. So I did some research before making my own poster.

It turns out that the original poster was the third in a series of three whose goal was to boost morale in the UK at the beginning of World War II. The British Ministry of Information printed 2.5 million copies of the Keep Calm and Carry On poster in 1939 to have on hand in the case of an invasion of Great Britain. The idea was to encourage people to keep on with their normal daily lives as if nothing had happened. And since the invasion never happened, the poster was never distributed, and instead the copies were destroyed.

Nobody knew a thing about it until 2000, the year in which two copies appeared in a box in a used bookstore in Northumberland in the north of England. Rediscovering the poster was like dusting off a forgotten piece of British history. It unleashed a torrent of media coverage, followed by its inevitable commercial exploitation. The poster quickly became a global icon.

The austere design of the poster, the confidence exuded by the crown of the Tudor King George VI, the clear, impelling message of the call to action—written with a simple typography—and the fact that the designer is an unknown (a forgotten civil servant) all give it a special mystique.

A message that is a call to action, that everyone can make their own, from a user (Great Britain) that has a considerable social reputation, published on its public (timeline), and that fits in 140 characters? That's a tweet if ever I saw one.

Viral

Soon after I published the tweet, still on the train, I realized that the message "Keep Calm and Speak Catalan" had taken off. It was soon to follow the general path of all those messages that go viral: Twitter and social media, blogs, digital newspapers, radio, television, printed editions of newspapers, and then round again.

The poster "Keep Calm and Speak Catalan" appears on websites in Japan and France, in protest movements in the United States, on websites in favor of Catalan culture and independence in Catalonia, as the avatars of thousands of Facebook and Twitter users, and at its peak had reached almost one million Google results (still nearly 800,000 as I write this article).

But almost at the same time as the tweet was spreading through the internet, it also started appearing in the real world, sometimes in the most unlikely places: as a poster for the Catalan beer maker Moritz, on t-shirts, posters, refrigerator magnets, pins, towels, mugs, blankets, and even fancy Munich sneakers (a Catalan brand whose shoes are sold worldwide). There was even a "Keep Calm and Speak Catalan Bus Tour" all over Catalonia.

Yes, the tweet got really, really big, both in and beyond the internet until the point in which in a session of the Spanish Congress a week later, during the debate on the very education reform bill that had originated the tweet, two MPs from the Catalan Parliamentary Group ERC brought a copy of the poster with them, and showed it to the Minister of Education from the podium. In that same session, a Catalan MP from an entirely different party (the social-democratic Unió Democràtica) finished his speech to the Minister with an additional definitive, "Keep Calm and Speak Catalan".

The whole experience was like earning a Masters in Communication in social networking, political communication, and marketing, all in the space of a single week.

Those Catalans are crazy

But why would a tweet that is little more than one more adaption of a British resistance slogan—and that says something so obvious like you should speak your own language—get so much play? Would it have had the same impact if instead of "Speak Catalan" we had put, say, "Speak French", "Spanish", "Italian", or "English"? I assure you, it would not have.

The tweet only worked because its target was a language that has been relegated to minority status and which finds itself in a struggle for recognition both in its own social and geographic sphere as well as in the global village in which we live. Advocating speaking a language that already enjoyed full health as well as the prestige and status as a global tool for communication would have come off as exclusive and authoritarian, even colonial. Recent history has some examples, like "Soyez propre, parlez Français" [Be clean, speak French], the French campaign to belittle the other "regional" languages in France. And "Hable en cristiano" [Speak in Christian], Spain's own effort to position Spanish above the other languages spoken in the Spanish State.

In the United States, Great Britain, or Italy, such a message would probably have been criticized by its own speakers. In Québec, Scotland, Ireland, and Flanders, it would not have.

My tweet, therefore, found fertile ground and a complicit audience, conscious that its language and culture live in a constant socio-political state of emergency which make something that is normal in any other corner of the world—that is, speaking, studying, and expressing oneself in the language of one's own country—something that needs constant justification. But that's nothing new.

A story

I was born in 1965 in a Catalan-speaking family. I spent my whole childhood in a small town called Tàrrega, of about 10,000 inhabitants in the hinterlands of Catalonia where almost everyone else was Catalan-speaking as well. In my class of 40 kids at school, there was a single Spanish speaker, and all of us spoke to him in Spanish. At home, with my friends, and when we played outside, everything was in Catalan, but our movies, TV, and comic books were in Spanish. At recess, things were more complicated: games and sports were in Spanish but role playing—say, Zorro or Batman—was in Spanish just the way they were in the movies or on television.

School was even more curious. While our books and school materials were all in Spanish, the younger teachers, from the town or close by, held their classes in Catalan without thinking twice about it (math, history, even Spanish language classes). The older teachers, even though they were also Catalans, changed to Spanish out of habit at the beginning of class, and switched back to Catalan at the end.

I remember perfectly well the language textbook from second grade that showed a map of Spain with the Spanish language and its three "dialects": Catalan, Basque, and Galician!

Little by little, with the arrival of democracy to Spain in 1975, Catalan found its natural space in the classroom and in high school; my classes were given in either Catalan or Spanish according to nothing more than the preference of each teacher. But now at least, we had Catalan language class, in which we learned that there are dialects of Classic Latin, like Spanish, Galician, and Portuguese, and dialects of Modern Latin, like Catalan, French, or Italian.

In high school, I studied other subjects, including French, Catalan, and Spanish, and I ended up taking the same university placement test that all of the students in the rest of the Spanish State took, as well as Catalan language and literature. And I passed them all, without any trouble. So a boy from a Spanish-speaking area of Spain, say, Seville, and I had the same possibilities of getting into university. The only difference was that I knew one language more.

I started college in 1983 and again the linguistic criteria for each class was the same: preference of the professor. In Catalan, I took algebra, probability, and statistics, computer theory, graph and combinatorial theory and lots more classes related with computer science. The bibliography, however, was all in English, and while I studied the material, I learned, almost without realizing it, this new language.

It was also in 1983 that the Government of Catalonia—with exclusive jurisdiction over educational matters—decided that all Catalan children would be educated in Catalan, regardless of their maternal language, so that they would not be segregated by mother tongue or origin. The Law of Linguistic Normalization, whose fundamental pillar was linguistic immersion, was passed. Students are immersed in the language that is used as the language of instruction—Catalan—and they also learn Spanish, a third language like English, and optionally, even a fourth.

This model has guaranteed that all Catalan students, regardless of their mother tongue, have, at the end of high school, the same level of Catalan that they do in Spanish, and that the level of Spanish of the Catalan students is comparable to the level of the rest of the students in the Spanish-speaking areas of Spain. The Catalan linguistic model has been recognized by the European Union for its success in the area of teaching in multilingual communities.

Problem? What problem?

If the real, measurable situation is that all Catalan students, regardless of their maternal language, are equally good at Spanish as anyone else—and in addition they know Catalan—where is the linguistic problem? Why do we have to change a model that has been working perfectly well for 30 years and which has been recognized by the European educational community?

I believe that when Groucho Marx said "Politics is the art of looking for trouble, finding it everywhere, diagnosing it incorrectly and applying the wrong remedies", he was thinking about Spain.

The Spanish State, conscious of the strong feelings of identity that language evokes in people, has always looked upon the non-Castilian languages and cultures of the State as a historic anomaly instead of considering them a common cultural patrimony that should be preserved and protected.

Take a look at just this one example (out of a multitude) from an extract from the "Secret instructions" that the attorney for the Council of Castile, don José Rodrigo Villalpando, wrote to the magistrates in Catalonia, way back on January 29, 1716:

> *". . . but since every Nation feels like its particular language is a gift of Nature, it makes them tricky to conquer and you need some time to do it, and even more when the people are, as in the case of the Catalans, tenacious, arrogant, and a lover of things from their own country, and for this reason, it's convenient to give careful thought out and concealed instructions and advice, so that the objective is obtained without being noticed . . ."*

However, this centralizing vocation has always come up against steadfast Catalan opposition, particularly in the last few years. Indeed, secessionism has risen in Catalonia and currently is polling at 57 percent in favor (January 21, 2013). On September 11, 2012, on Catalonia's National Day, 1.5 million people (out of a total population of 7 million) marched in favor of the independence of Catalonia and to be the next state in Europe.

This demonstration had consequences at the Spanish level as well as the Catalan. How could so many people come out all of a sudden when other year's demonstrations only garnered 60,000 attendees? Where did this movement come from?

The Spanish Minister of Education was convinced that he knew: 30 years of indoctrination of Catalan children—with a "twisted" account of history full of "false" myths about Catalonia's glorious past—had begun to bear fruit, and it was time to put an end to it. To hammer home his message in the Spanish Congress of Deputies, he declared that it was his and the government's intention to "hispanicize" Catalan schoolchildren.

The Spanish Minister of Education's reform bill revolves around the supposed right of parents to choose the language in which their children would be educated. For the Minister, the law should allow Spanish-speaking parents in Catalonia to be able to choose Spanish as the language of instruction for their child, and to study Catalan as if it were a foreign language.

Can the preferences of the parents override the criteria of pedagogues, teachers, and institutions on what should be studied and what their children will learn? In Spain, it seems so.

Despite being absolutely opposed to the Minister's unique way of thinking and his diagnosis of the situation, I couldn't agree more with his analysis. It was McLuhan who said the medium is the message, and the act of teaching in one language or another, the act of putting the focus on a territory or another, and the act of giving more importance to one historical episode or another changes the vision we have of reality. Spain's history, which the minister worries so much about, does not come out the same when explained in Catalan, in English, or in Spanish, and it's not the same if the story is told from Catalonia, from Latin America, or from Portugal.

The minister deliberately forgets that a single, objective "history" does not exist; the only histories that exist are biased ones written by the victors. And not even these are constant since the way they are seen and interpreted changes with the times. Or does the minister not remember when Catalan was a "dialect" of Spanish in those textbooks?

Until lions have their historians, tales of the hunt shall always glorify the hunter, I assure you.

The future

Many media interpreted "Keep Calm and Speak Catalan" as a reaction to the Spanish government's attitude toward the Catalan education system. That's a part of it, but there is much more. Whoever thinks that my tweet and the reaction to it were simply the product of the collective reaction to the Spanish minister's law—one in a long line of such initiatives—is wrong indeed.

The success of the message only became possible because it resonated with thousands of sympathetic Catalans who, upon retweeting, wearing the t-shirt, or putting on the sneakers, made the message their own and then passed it on, conscious of the need to react clearly, intelligently, and definitively to the constant and recurring supremacist will of Spanish over Catalan. Unfortunately, the success of my tweets is proof that such a will exists.

My Catalan-speaking parents were never allowed to learn how to write Catalan at school and the love letters they sent to each other had to be written in a language that was not their own. Imagine sending a postcard to a loved one in the language of your neighboring country and you will quickly see how absurd that is. Fortunately, my son will learn the language of his grandparents in total normalcy at a public school in our own country.

I hope that very soon a slogan like "Keep Calm and Speak Catalan" gets no play at all.

Wilson, Obama, Catalonia, and Figueres

Enric Pujol Casademont

Ph.D. in History from the Autonomous University of Barcelona. Pujol has authored, coauthored and managed several books, the latest of which is Història i reconstrucció nacional [History and National Reconstruction] *(2003). Among other projects, he carried out the museological and museographical project of the Exile Museum of La Jonquera (2002–2007) with Jaume Santaló. He served as coordinator of the History and Contemporary Thought Area of the Presidential Department of the Government of Catalonia (2005–2007). He is currently a professor at the Autonomous University of Barcelona and is a member of the Governing Board of the Democratic Memorial of the Government of Catalonia.*

The relationship between the United States and Catalonia throughout the contemporary period has been all over the map. There have been dark moments with tension and there have been wonderful inspiring moments of great confidence and hope. Some day, not too far off, it will be necessary to write a detailed account of the relationship between our two peoples that, despite the ties that we have maintained, requires much more coverage than it's gotten to date. Here and now, however, I'll limit myself to remarking on two completely opposite episodes: two extremes.

We'll begin with an event that could be included in what we've called the "dark times": the conflict motivated by the colonial war between Cuba and the Spanish State at the end of the 19th century. On that occasion, the United States supported Cuban independence, while Catalonia gave all its support to the Spanish government (because in practice, Cuba had functioned as a Catalan colony). There was, therefore, a stark conflict of interests that left its mark on the Catalan mentality of the era. Just a few years later, however, things changed radically.

The loss of Cuba and of the Philippines at the end of the 1800s by the Spanish State had a huge if indirect effect on Catalan society which, all of a sudden, became aware of the State's inability to confront the great challenges of the new 20th century that were buffeting Catalonia and on which she depended. It was around the same time that the modern Catalanist movement took off, hoping to achieve recognition of some kind of self-government that would serve as a way of constructing a very few minimum structures of state. The basic objective was to be able to ensure its continuity as a national community, with its own language and culture, that wished to be part of one of the most established ones (materially and spiritually speaking) in the Europe of the era.

The struggle with the Spanish government over this goal was arduous but it bore some notable fruit in the moments leading up to World War I. And here is where we come to a second moment, one that is brighter, in the relationship between the two countries. In 1914, we were able to establish the first Catalan self-government since 1714, which was called the *Mancomunitat* de Catalonia. It was, above all, a huge if symbolic event, since the actual political jurisdiction it had was very limited. Precisely because of those limitations, the demand for more important powers continued unabated. There was, therefore, great national turmoil, which coincided with the first worldwide armed conflict of the 20th century, during which Spain maintained a position of neutrality.

From Catalonia, there were demands for Madrid to allow a statute—a kind of constitution—that would recognize the existing self-government and that would extend its jurisdiction. But these majority demands from the Catalan people were ignored by the Spanish government at which point the voices got much louder and much more open, demanding Catalan independence.

At the end of the world war, the groups that spoke out in favor of the right of self-determination for Catalonia lived moments of high hopes, precisely thanks to the international positioning that was adopted, on that occasion, by the president of the United States, Woodrow Wilson (1856–1924). The general trauma unleashed by that war had been so great that there was a very extensive feeling around the world that an experience as devastating as a war of worldwide proportions could never happen again. Fully conscious of the situation, President Wilson proposed a program of 14 basic points that were meant to make it impossible for Europe and the rest of the world to ever go to war again. Out of the 14, one of these points had particular resonance for Catalonia, since it proposed the recognition of the right of a people to self-determination.

Different Catalan groups, both on the left and the right, saw in the American leader's statements a legitimation of their aspirations for achieving the full sovereignty of our country. And enthusiasm broke out all over. Even today, almost 100 years after the fact, there are material reminders of the great hope that took hold in various places in the country. One of these physical reminders can be found in Figueres, my home town. It's a small city with not quite 50,000 inhabitants, a few kilometers from the border of the French Republic, and which has become internationally famous as the birthplace of painter Salvador Dalí, and for housing the principal museum dedicated to his work.

In the time of the Wilson declaration, the city was ruled, and had been for some time, by leftist republicans, who were ardent supporters of Catalan self-determination. The admiration that the Wilson declaration awoke in Figueres was so great that they decided to hire a prestigious sculptor, Frederic Marès, to build a monument dedicated to the American president. The sculpture, that is still displayed publicly to this day, is a very elegant bust, in 19th-century style, and represents a woman with a classic tunic and Phrygian cap with her left hand holding up a torch. The symbolic references to a Catalan Republic are quite clear. Next to the figure there is this inscription: "Peoples must be neither tamed nor governed, except with their own consent".

In 1918, the sculpture was installed on one of the most central streets in the city, which from that moment forward was called President Wilson Avenue.

During the military dictatorship of General Francisco Franco (1939–1975), the monument's message was interpreted by the totalitarian regime as clearly subversive, and the sculpture was taken down. Luckily it was not destroyed, but instead left in a municipal warehouse for untold years. It wasn't until the end of the dictatorship, in the second half of the 1970s, that the piece was placed again in the public space. And it wasn't until 2004 that it was situated in its current position, next to some municipal buildings on the general thoroughfare.

Unfortunately, Wilson didn't receive a lot of support for carrying out his projects for world peace. A new international war, even more devastating than the previous one, broke out just a few years later. Catalonia was unsuccessful then as well in having her national aspirations recognized and she was forced to live under a military dictatorship that lasted forty years, during which not only was she refused any kind of self-government, but the Catalan language and culture were also systematically persecuted.

Not too long ago, on September 25, 2012, President Barack Obama made an unrelated statement on the right of self-determination: "we believe freedom and self determination are not unique to one culture . . . they are universal values". Now it would be nice if an effort were made to spell out and politically recognize this right of the Catalan people. If such a thing happened, I'm sure that the enthusiasm that existed at the beginning of the last century would look small next to the reaction that such a declaration would get today. Without a doubt, we are at the highest, most hopeful point in the relationship between our two nations. Perhaps if someone could explain to Mr. Obama this small story of our shared history, he might decide to take such a step. Our confidence and our hope as a people are in his hands.

News from Catalonia

Josep M. Muñoz

Historian and editor. Ph.D. in Contemporary History from the University of Barcelona. Muñoz is the author of Jaume Vicens i Vives (1910–1960): una biografia intel·lectual [Jaume Vicens i Vives: An Intellectual biography] *(1997). He has held a variety of professional positions, and since 2000 is the editor of a cultural monthly magazine,* L'Avenç, *and the related tiny publishing house that publishes books on history and literature.*

In 1954, right in the middle of General Franco's dictatorship, the most European Spanish historian of the moment, the Catalan Jaume Vicens Vives, published a book that was destined to make a small fortune. The conditions in which it was written and published were that of harsh censorship, in which many things could not be called by their proper names. To start with, Vicens Vives had originally titled his work *We the Catalans* but he was obliged to change it to the more innocuous *News from Catalonia*. Only 15 years had passed since the end of the devastating civil war and the Catalans, defeated as a people, needed to know "who they were" before they could move into the future.

In 1960, Vicens reedited his small book. He added new chapters, products of the evolution of his own thought processes. In particular, he now focused his reflections on the relationship that, historically, the Catalans had established with the structures of power. Using the metaphor of the Minotaur, Vicens considered that since Catalonia had been integrated into the Spanish monarchy, Catalans had gotten out of the habit of being in power, which they saw as something more and more foreign. Vicens had described in his books the evolution of Catalonia as two sides of the same coin: the decadence of the 15th century, with the consequent loss of the political "charter for navigation", had been followed by a renaissance that began in the economic sphere and followed in the political and cultural.

In that way, the 19th century in Catalonia—known precisely as the *Renaixença* or renaissance, in which Catalonia ended up transformed into "Spain's factory"—was characterized by a decided desire of the Catalans, who up to that moment had been kept away from power, to intervene in Spanish affairs. Catalonia wanted to fashion Spain after itself, which was nothing more, according to Vicens, than another way of being European. That is, the Catalans wanted to modernize and Europeanize a backward Spain, which was in the hands of the dominant Castilian classes which socially and economically had little to do with the industrialization that Catalonia had experienced. Therefore, for a period of years the Catalan industrialists and politicians proposed various ways that Spain could recognize Catalonia's singularity, at the same time as it attempted to construct an efficient Spanish State. *Political Catalanism*, the name that this movement ended up adopting, was always a movement that simultaneously tried to regenerate Spain.

But Catalonia found it very difficult to have its proposals for *regeneration* accepted. The crisis of 1898, in which Spain had lost the last remains of its old colonial empire on the other side of the ocean after a humiliating defeat at the hands of the United States, convinced many Catalans of the practical impossibility of that "fashioning" or modernizing. Catalonia instead turned back on itself. Vicens underlines how the two great social and political movements at the turn of the 20th century in Catalonia saw both a bourgeois Catalanism and a working class anarchism, which shared a common mistrust of the Spanish State and the real possibility of effectively modernizing it.

The history of the 20th century has not been very different in some respects. Catalonia has continued to be one of the economic powerhouses of Spain (it represents 16 percent of the total Spanish population, 20 percent of its GDP, and 26 percent of its exports). It has continued to struggle to fashion Spain in its own image, and to establish a framework for peaceful coexistence that started with its recognition as a linguistic and cultural reality, as well as a differentiated social and political one. In 20th-century Spain, there has been no democracy without a simultaneous recognition of the right of Catalans to self-government, and there has no been no dictatorship without a simultaneous repression or prohibition of this right. That is, the century began with a meek attempt at self-governance in the form of the *Mancomunitat* of Catalonia of 1914, which was overturned in 1923 by the dictatorship of General Primo de Rivera. The Second Republic was born in 1931 with the explicit agreement that led to the Statute of Autonomy of the Catalans, which was approved (not without many reservations from the Spanish Jacobins) in 1932.

The long dictatorship of General Franco, which lasted until his death in 1975, was the result of a bloody civil war (1936–1939) that began with a military coup d'état. One of the causes of the coup was the adamant opposition that the civil forces that began and supported the *putsch* felt toward the self-governing Statute of the Catalans, which was immediately suppressed. One of the results of the dictatorship was the dramatic prohibition of the public use of the Catalan language and the attempt, which failed in the end, but was not for that reason any less damaging, of annihilating its culture. Out of the Franco dictatorship came a negotiated process known as the "Democratic Transition", a product of which was the Spanish Constitution of 1978, which was known, perhaps with some exaggeration, as the "Constitution of the Catalans" thanks to the responsibility that some Catalan politicians had, both from the left and the right, in its drafting.

The State of the Autonomies, described in the Constitution of 1978, meant a recognition of the plurality of the Spanish State, but it left many areas undefined, with many ambiguities. Another historian, the Frenchman Pierre Vilar, harshly qualified it as "artifice rather than edifice". Still, the edifice has sheltered, imperfectly, with more or less constant tension, the demands of most Catalans during 25 years. At the beginning of the 21st century, however, its limits became clear: the Statute of Autonomy approved in 1979 within the framework of the Spanish Constitution was not sufficient to hold back the "recentralizing" will with which the Spanish democratic governments, once the Transition was over, focused their vision of how the new Spanish State should be articulated.

In particular, the operation (begun by the right with the implicit acquiescence of the left) of pivoting the new state around its capital, Madrid, was transformed into not just the political capital it had been for centuries, but above all into the center of Spanish financial power. It brought about the design and articulation of a radial design where everything begins and ends in the center—"Great Madrid". The political mistrust toward the two traditional industrial poles of the peninsula—Catalonia and the Basque Country—was clearly implicit in this bet on the "radial Spain", a bet that had its maximum expression in the grandiose network of high-speed railways that began to be built during the years of illusory plenty. (And about which a high-ranking American statesman exclaimed, "We're not wealthy enough to pay for something like that!" Soon it would become clear that the Spaniards weren't either.)

Meanwhile, the feeling began to grow, weakly at the onset but fully part of the mainstream now, that the contribution that Catalonia makes to the Spanish coffers does not have a sufficient corresponding return in the form of investments or infrastructures. Since "radial Spain" was constructed contrary to economic logic and instead only for political reasons, Spain has neglected its Mediterranean flank, which paradoxically, is where the bulk of its exporting power is located. In that way, in the name of interterritorial solidarity, the trains have been modernized while the engine car has been weakened. The result is that the whole train goes much more slowly, with one of the engineers fuming that they're withholding his coal.

Faced with this situation, the majority of Catalan political forces tried to shield the self-government's jurisdictions (or *reserved matters*, if you will) with a reform of the Statute of Autonomy approved in 2006. The process was full of incidents, and ended quite badly. The People's Party (a pro-Spanish rightist party, which is a minority party in Catalonia) brought the new Statute to the discredited Spanish Constitutional Court, despite the fact that it had been approved by both the Catalan and Spanish parliaments and by the citizens of Catalonia in a referendum. The ruling of this high court, with pressure from multiple angles that dragged out the process until 2010, delegitimized the foundations of the Catalans' self-government, and seemed to cut off the path that the Spanish Constitution of 1978 had opened.

Currently, a remarkably wide majority of Catalans have defended, on the streets and at the polls, their "right to decide". This stems directly from this ruling, and from Spain's desire to "recentralize" power in both the economic and political terrains. The latest polls say that 57 percent of the registered voters would vote right now for Catalonia to become "a new state in Europe".

What has brought us to this point? Keep in mind that independentism has never before garnered majority support in Catalonia, not even among openly nationalist forces. I think I can sum it up this way: in the same way that the American Colonies rebelled against the power of the British with the slogan "No taxation without representation", today a substantial portion of Catalans, whose motives are more democratic than strictly nationalist, are saying no to an excessive fiscal imposition and to a clearly insufficient recognition of their political rights. The inability of the Spanish State to confront the Catalan question, by giving them political recognition or the financial sufficiency which Catalans demand, is what has made many (though not all) Catalans say today, "Goodbye, Spain".

On the prickly matter of language

J.C. Major

New York-based linguist. Major is co-founder of the Col·lectiu Emma (Emma Network), an opinion group about Catalan issues, and chief editorial writer for its website, "Explaining Catalonia".

"The importance of making the language uniform has always been recognized as great, and it is a sign of dominion or superiority by princes or nations . . ."
José Rodrigo Villalpando, senior officer of the Council of Castile, 1716

"The utmost resolve shall be applied in introducing the Castilian language, to which end the most guarded and surreptitious measures should be taken, so that the effect is accomplished without the intent being noticed."
From the secret instructions issued to government officials deployed in Catalonia, 1717

"It is our interest to 'hispanicize' Catalan children."
José Ignacio Wert, Spain's Minister of Education, 2012

What, then, makes a nation? Not race or religion—at least not for Catalans. Nor the trappings of power—a state, an army—whose unquestioned benefits they lost a long time ago. The right place to look for proof of Catalonia's unique personality is in the broad field of culture—in the set of values and customs that are shared by a community and are specific to it, the common way of doing things that is recognized as such by the people living in a certain land and also by those coming into contact with it for the first time.

Catalans are no different from any other society in the world in that their culture has a particular language as its proper vehicle. And, no differently from every other society in the world, they see in their language a central element of their national character. This should be easy enough to understand. And yet, a common criticism of Catalans is that they give too much importance to their language. That is chiefly because, in spite of its remarkable past as a self-governing nation, of having preserved to this day its distinctive culture and of having belatedly recovered a fraction of its political institutions, Catalonia is not thought about as an independent community but merely as part of something else. To be sure, if Catalans are defined as only a subset of the general Spanish population, their insistence on speaking something different from the rest may be seen as an anomaly. And a silly one to boot. Wouldn't they be better off, a pragmatic outsider might reasonably ask, if they restricted their local tongue to family use or gave it up altogether to embrace their neighbors' formidable language, which they all know anyway? Castilian is, after all, official in Spain, the state that most Catalans belong to, and they're all required by law to learn it. It is also the first language of more than 300 million people, most of them in Latin America, and has roughly 35 million native speakers in Spain alone. Catalan, with an area of some 10 million altogether, is certainly small by comparison, and has a more limited reach. So it would be justifiable to think that Catalans may really be overdoing it when they make all that fuss about their relatively unimportant language.

But just stop to consider for a second in what way Catalans are behaving differently from other linguistic communities in Europe. Do the 6 million Finns, for instance, who are sitting next to 170 million Russian speakers and keep on nattering away in Finnish regardless, set too much store on their language or just the right amount? And what about the 5.5 million Danes, living their merry lives speaking Danish just a stone's throw away from one of Europe's economic powerhouses that is home to almost 82 million German speakers? What sets Catalans apart from those other smaller nations? You may have guessed it: the only difference lies in the fact that Finns and Danes, being masters of their own lands, don't have to compete with a neighbor's language in them. But, wouldn't a Finn or a Dane be preoccupied with his or her language if it were forced to coexist with that of a more powerful society which has long had total political control over their territories? And this is precisely the Catalans' lot: to have been engulfed in a political structure run by another national group with a history of aggressively pushing its own language and customs in every land it has ever acquired—by whatever means.

Casual observers may not be aware of the lengths that official Spain has gone to in order to thrust the Castilian language upon peoples that had never felt the need for it. The fact is that at every point in history and under every kind of government, laws and regulations have been issued aiming to dislodge languages other than Castilian from all spheres of life outside private and family communication. Thus, the presence of Castilian in Catalonia can in no way be put down to a natural process of substitution, where a weaker and presumably more inadequate language gradually gives way to a stronger and better equipped one, but should be considered primarily the result of a strategy of assimilation applied by the State.

Two conclusions can be drawn from all this. One belongs to the Spanish narrative and posits that, considering the political reality and the subordinate status of Catalonia within Spain, Catalans should have given up their language in favor of Castilian, which, under the loftier name of Spanish, was declared compulsory for all the peoples of a vast empire and now boasts for that reason a large number of speakers. In the normal course of events, and given the obvious asymmetry between the two contenders, Catalan should have gone the way of so many native languages that have died out or are just clinging to life as inferior alternatives to Spanish in the part of America that was compelled to become Latin.

The other opposite conclusion is that the Catalan language—together with the culture whose means of expression it is and the society that it serves—must have some intrinsic value if it has been able to withstand the competition against such an exalted rival. All the more so if one considers the degree of force applied by the other side in order to suppress it. In fact, given the almost impossible odds and the hard resolve of its enemies, it is surprising that Catalan has been able to remain alive at all—and, by the look of it, in fairly good health. Still, an uneventful life can't be guaranteed even in our seemingly milder times. There may not be open persecution today—in 2012 people don't get slapped in public for speaking in Catalan, as was the rule in the early nineteen-forties, and not an unheard-of risk as late as the sixties—but this doesn't mean that the existence of the Catalan language—or, indeed, of the Catalan nation—has been accepted into the official Spanish worldview. On the contrary, every small gain made by Catalans on the linguistic front will be resisted as just another dent in the position of dominance that Spaniards enjoy in Catalonia.

Spain has a history of never playing fair with Catalans, including on the subject of their language, and it simply couldn't act differently so late in the game. Every new season brings fresh examples of subtle and not-so-subtle attacks suggesting that it won't let up on its obsession to undermine the language as a way of wiping out the nation. So for Catalans, today as much as ever, working to safeguard their language is a matter of survival.

Is the perfect always and everywhere the enemy of the good?

Edward Hugh

Independent macroeconomist, specializing in growth and productivity theory, with particular emphasis on the economic impacts of aging populations and other demographic processes like migration flows. Best known internationally for his writings on the Spanish economic crises, and his participation in the Latvian devaluation debate, Hugh is also an expert on the European Sovereign Debt Crisis and a member of the board of directors of the bank Catalunya Caixa. He is a regular contributor to a number of widely read weblogs, including A Fistful of Euros, Roubini Global Economics Monitor, and Demography Matters, and maintains an active and dynamic Facebook community.

Against a backdrop which offers an eerie parallel with events that took place somewhat to the north more than 30 years ago, Catalonia is now threatening to separate from Spain. In so doing the region seems to be putting at risk both the future of the host country and beyond that the outlook for the Euro currency and the process of European unification.

The parallel is of course with the drive for Baltic independence and its impact on Mikhail Gorbachev's ill-fated attempt to peacefully reform the disintegrating Soviet Union. In the words of Aleksandr Yakovlev, one of his closest associates at the time, the ideas of those seeking independence were "out of touch with reality" and any expectation that the Baltic republics could regain the independent status they had before Soviet annexation in 1940 was "simply unrealistic." As late as February 1991, Gorbachev himself was still describing the Lithuanian vote—described by the countries leaders as simply a non-binding opinion poll—as illegal, and this a matter of days before it was actually held.

Sound familiar? It should, since these very same arguments are now being played out in another pole of Europe. Not only is the Spanish administration taking precisely the view that any vote in Catalonia on whether or not to separate from Spain would be illegal, the attitudes of those outside the country are largely being conditioned, not by the merits or otherwise of the Catalan case, but by the fear of what might happen to Spain if Catalonia left.

While Catalans busy themselves assuring each other that any new state would be economically viable, few on the outside doubt that this would be the case. To give but one example, former chief economist at the IMF Kenneth Rogoff recently commented that Catalonia on its own constitutes one of the richest regions in Europe. This is simply stating the obvious. What has external observers really worried is the subsequent viability of Spain, and with it the future of the euro. If Spain is too big to be allowed to fail, then Catalonia is too small to have inalienable rights, the argument seems to run.

It is for this reason, I feel, that the Catalan cause is attracting little sympathy beyond the confines of what is often called the "Principality".

Many feel that Catalonia is being selfish—just as they felt in their day that the citizens of the Baltics were—in putting their own particularist interests (a better fiscal distribution, the right to a national football team) before those of the collective (economic recovery, closer political union in Europe, and so on). But this way of looking at things is essentially flawed, just as it was in Estonia, Latvia, and Lithuania. The movement for Catalan independence is primarily, and at its core, a democratic one. So what should matter to the outside world is not whether the vote will be considered legal by the central government in Madrid, or whether the Catalans have a good case. If the Catalans vote peacefully and democratically, and by a significant majority, that they want to form a separate state, then it is clear that the region's days inside the frontiers of the Kingdom of Spain are numbered. Unless, that is, the Catalans be retained within those frontiers by the use of force, in which case some of the fundamental principles of the Treaty of Europe will be put in question. Hence the fundamental dilemma that the Catalan independence drive presents to the whole European Union.

Under these circumstances what outside observers should focus on is what the result of the vote will be. After all, what the Catalans are demanding at the moment is "the right to decide", and at the end of the day it is they who will decide. My country, as the saying goes, right or wrong.

Nothing here is either unavoidable or inevitable. As in the case of Greek euro exit, beyond the expedient there are no ex ante juridical limits to the bounds of the possible. What is important for everyone is that the eventual solution be an orderly one.

In this context messages that the new country, should one be created, would need to apply for membership of the European Union constitute nothing more than mere hot air, just as the suggestions from the Spanish administration that any such application would be met with a veto on their part is no more than an empty threat. Such talk is not in the realm of the real, or the realistic. It is simply an attempt to alter the outcome of the vote, and a bad and ineffective one at that. Not for nothing does Catalonia's President Mas describe the speechwriters of the Partido Popular as running a production line for manufacturing separatists.

If Spain's sovereign debt is already on an unsustainable path, then how much less sustainable would it become if the country suddenly had its GDP reduced by 20 percent? Common sense dictates that negotiations would be held, negotiations in which Catalonia would be asked to accept a proportion of the legacy debt, just as common sense suggests that Catalonia's financial system, which has assets of approximately 500 billion euros (in other words, it is much larger than the Greek equivalent) would be allowed to remain in the eurosystem. The alternatives—and their consequences well beyond the frontiers of Europe—are simply unthinkable.

Naturally sometimes the unthinkable happens, especially when a majority of the key players assume it won't. Catalonia has now decided to hold some sort of "consultation" or "opinion poll" during 2014. As in the Lithuanian case, the outcome may not be binding, but few should draw comfort from that single fact and assume that the result will not be significant and even decisive for the short-term future of Europe.

As I say, nothing here is inevitable, or foretold in advance. But avoiding predestination involves facing up to the facts, and not, as the IMF Director General Christine Lagarde recently put it in the Greek context, engaging in wishful thinking. And the facts in this case are that dialogue between Catalonia and the rest of Spain has now broken down. Catalans are tired of not being listened to, while the rest of Spain is tired of the Catalans and their constant demands for more autonomy. At one pole there is "Spain weariness" and at the other "Catalonia exhaustion". Matters have now gone past the point where orderly solutions will be sought out and found internally.

Most external observers expected some sort of offer to be made by the central government after the Catalan elections, but reading the result as a setback and defeat for President Mas, the only "offer" which has been sent to Barcelona is one which involves "hispanicizing" children via the reform of the Catalan education system, a move which has effectively united the Catalans behind their new government. That is why a decisive intervention on the part of Europe's political leaders is crucial. Whether they like it or not they now have no alternative but to become intermediaries in the search for viable solutions. If not, neglect will only produce the result everyone seeks to avoid.

It is no accident that the Baltics saw their chance just in the moment of maximum Russian weakness, and that Catalans see their only realistic possibility of achieving their objective of having their own state just when Spain is effectively on the ropes, and possibly in terminal decline. Some, comforted by the writings of Francis Fukuyama, feel that what is happening to Spain is simply an unfortunate setback on the bumpy road to becoming a mature democracy, but darker readings are possible. This crisis is not simply cyclical or conjunctural and there is a real possibility that the country's problems are so complex that it will become impossible for Spain's leaders to fix them without recourse to an Argentina-style default. It is precisely the loss of confidence in the capacity of the Spanish political class to resolve the country's dire economic situation, and the mounting frustration with their perpetual insistence that all will be well starting tomorrow that has the Catalans running for the exit door. If the building is about to burn down they don't want to be trapped inside when it happens. As Janice Joplin once put it, freedom is sometimes "just another word for having nothing left to lose".

In the critical weeks and months that are to come, I think it is important that all participants bear in mind that once the Baltic vote was taken, and once the demise of Gorbachev became inevitable, attitudes toward the new countries rapidly changed. All three are now consolidated members of the European Union, and the past is simply that, what is over. Many Catalans tell me they are doing what they are doing, not for themselves but for their children and their grandchildren. A few years of economic turbulence, measured on such a time scale, seems like nothing. In the interest of the common good, solutions need to be found—solutions which are able to both satisfy the aspirations of the Catalans and guarantee stability in Europe. If this search is not initiated soon, then time will ineluctably run out and the likely will steadily become the inevitable. Simple application of the rules of game theory tell us that. There isn't a day to lose. You know it makes sense.

What has happened to us Catalans?

Salvador Cardús

Ph.D. in Economics, Autonomous University of Barcelona (UAB). Visiting researcher at the University of Cambridge, Cornell University, and Queen Mary College of London. Professor of Sociology at the UAB. Research in sociology of religion, media and communication, and identity. Cardús has published, among other things, Plegar de viure [Giving up on Living] *with Joan Estruch,* Saber el temps [Knowing Time], *and* El camí de la independència [The Road to Independence]. *Former deputy director of the daily Avui (1989–1991). Columnist for* ARA, La Vanguardia, *and Catalunya Ràdio. Full member of the Institute for Catalan Studies (Catalonia's Sciences Academy).*

The interpretation of the past

It's not at all easy to explain to a reader who is unaware of the social, cultural, and political reality of Catalonia how Catalonia has gradually turned in favor of independence over the past few years. To someone who's new to the issue and not familiar with the historic or political background and who's intrigued about the immediate causes of a wish to break up a state, the shift would probably seem capricious, if not opportunist. Indeed, the lack of knowledge and perspective on the internal and peculiar situation makes the external and more general aspects, the more obvious ones, the more stereotypical, seem "natural". And when this "naturalness" doesn't live up to snuff, it's normal that instead of doubting if that stereotypical image was fictitious or forced, we demand explanations from those who revealed our ignorance.

The Catalans, right now, find ourselves in this predicament: to have to explain and justify that which is a profound reality of our country, and to defend it against stereotypes and misconceptions. Well, let's get to it! You first have to remember that throughout the 20th century the Francoist dictatorship assimilated us into an indivisible Spanish archetype all the while repressing any expression of cultural, linguistic, political, or economic difference. After the dictatorship, with the delicate Transition toward democracy, Catalonia's national ambitions were again masked. Everyone pretended that they were resolved by a political model called the "Spain of the Autonomies", the exaltation of which was necessary for consolidating the whole new democratic structure. So, we had 40 years of Spanishness forced on us by the dictatorship followed by 30 more with the promise that the democratic consolidation of Spain—if carried out peacefully— would allow Catalonia to evolve toward more developed forms of self-government and respect for our national reality. In total, for more than 70 years, they have hidden from the outside world the fact that we are a "different" society.

Yes, Catalonia is as much or more different than Scotland or Québec, but the political circumstances have hidden that fact. The old historic nation, the cultural and linguistic reality that is so different from Spain's, the will to recover the political liberties that were lost in the War of Succession of 1714—the true First World War—were all politically constrained by a wide regionalist nationalism and by a minority secessionism from an internal point of view, which internationally, only the culturally enlightened minorities were aware of.

Therefore, the first thing that we need to make clear is that everything that is happening in Catalonia is not coming from an unexpected burst of political madness, from ethnic xenophobia, or selfish parsimony exacerbated by the current financial crisis, but rather is the product of the maturation of historic aspirations. A process that has been, certainly, expressed in many different ways over the years, and that in this latest phase, for reasons I will attempt to expose, has the majority leaning toward a wish for having state structures—and if possible, staying within Europe—achieved peacefully and through a process of democratic self-determination. This expression of majority rule has not only surprised international public opinion, it also snuck up even on Spain, which has always belittled and underestimated Catalans' national aspirations. And so it was that Spain concluded that the autonomic model established by the Constitution of 1978 did not only resolve the historic aspirations of the Basques and Catalans, but trusted that these would be dissolved in a process of simple administrative decentralization.

The failure of the autonomic model

Nevertheless, that autonomic model that watered down the political ambitions of two historic nations into 17 administrative regions has failed on various fronts. On the one hand, because it has satisfied neither the aspirations of the Basques nor those of the Catalans—to different degrees and for reasons that would take too long to explain here. And on the other because Spanish nationalism, which is profoundly centralist and homogenizing, felt threatened by its own invention. The administrative decentralization introduced many economic and political inefficiencies into the system, and with good reason, the State felt weakened.

The resistance toward the autonomic process by the Spanish themselves could be felt from the very start—this was the principal motivation behind the coup d'état of 1981. In addition, in practice, legislation was passed with the express objective of invading the autonomies' areas of jurisdiction so that the central government could take them back. But it's true that the evolution from theory to practice of this anti-autonomism becomes most prevalent from 2000 on thanks to the conservative party, Partit Popular, and its president, José María Aznar. From that point forward, the failure of the autonomic model is not speculation from the vantage point of so-called Catalan victimization, but the pretext of a well-articulated program to take back established autonomic powers from several different statutes of autonomy.

From the Catalan side, the ample awareness of the failure of the autonomic model came a few years later. In 2004, when the Parliament of Catalonia began to reform the Statute of 1979 in which lay the foundations of political autonomy, there was little general awareness of the model's weakness in satisfying national expectations. At that point, the political parties were more aware of the weaknesses of the autonomies than the people were. When the reform was initiated, led by Pasqual Maragall, the objective was to manage to properly fit Catalonia into Spain by means of a federal system. For the CiU nationalists, the objective was the recognition of the Catalan national reality with special emphasis on equal treatment of the Catalan and Spanish languages—as official languages with the same rights and obligations—and on the modification of the model of regional financing. In the end, the ERC independentists supported the reform of the Statute trusting that it would mean the beginning of a new transition that would lead toward their own clearly secessionist goals.

But the Spanish Congress, on which the ratification of the Statutory reform depended, eliminated most of the significant improvements that were proposed for self-government in 2006. What is worse, the Constitutional Court ended up restrictively amending the new law, even though its whittled-down version had already been passed by referendum and received a rather resigned affirmative vote. Awareness of the complete failure of the project, which began to be clear in 2006, was widespread by 2010. The Catalan people leapfrogged the political class by demanding a new sovereigntist political framework. The final denouement arrived with the demonstration on September 11, 2012, the day that Catalonia celebrates its National Day.

At any rate, the part that is hardest to document in a brief and clear fashion is that which here I can only sustain as a hypothesis. And that is the fact that the triggering of secessionist feeling, which according to most rigorous polls has reached between 55 and 60 percent of the voting population, has to do with an unrelenting process of humiliation since 2006. I say that it's not easy to quickly demonstrate it because it has to do with a process of changing the emotional structure, fed especially by political provocations that often have more symbolic than legal force. Of course, it's undeniable that the financial crisis has also more clearly revealed the unfair fiscal treatment—the *plundering*, in political combat terms—and the mistreatment in public investments, a fact that has accompanied and reinforced this very notable political transformation.

Perspectives for the future

It's not hard to imagine, from a Catalan vantage point, the political collapse that this mainstream independentism has provoked in Spain. The reaction from the Spanish has been of the lowest democratic quality, unimaginable in any of the neighboring countries. The most common reactions have been threats and insults, and there has been no lack of dirty tricks. I won't enter into details here either, because it's not unlikely that this viscerality will become even more stark as the time for making a final decision gets closer. On the other hand, for the Catalans, what may be most surprising is the rather undramatic fashion in which the expectation of national emancipation is being experienced by most of the population. That is, the vote against the recognition of the right to self-determination of the Catalans held on to only 20 percent of the votes in the last elections (on November 25, 2012), and only 14 percent of the registered voters. One might even consider that this de-dramatization of the process' repercussions might reveal a certain unawareness of the seriousness of the proposal. But the truth is that the majority of independentists believe that they are simply availing themselves of a democratic right that does not deserve—given their peaceful character—the irritation with which it has been received. And suffice it to say that this lack of drama is most obvious among the youngest generations, who did not live through the Francoist past of the country, nor the transition to democracy, and therefore haven't developed any feelings of loyalty to a Spanish Constitution that they consider disloyal to Catalonia.

The whole situation is helped, of course, by the fact that the globalization process, though it may seem paradoxical, makes the advantages of a large state and wide borders increasingly irrelevant. It's clear that since the world is better and better connected, and more interdependent, independence poses no risk of isolation, especially in Europe where even physical borders are not an issue. It's for that reason that, in this context, Catalans take for granted that their independence makes total sense within the European Union, and not just in its current form, but also if it should end up becoming the United States of Europe, with a similar structure to the United States. In fact, it's little known that an independent Catalonia, would be ranked 13th by population among the 50 current states of the United States, and would occupy the 7th position of the 27 states of the European Union, or the 9th when ranked by GDP (according to the IMF, 2011).

The future of Catalonia is uncertain, and the fight is between the defense of the right of the state by the Spanish and the strength of the expression of the democratic will that many Catalans believe should be above and beyond any previous legality. We'll find out what's going to happen before two years are through.

Our place in the world: the country of Barcelona

Vicent Partal

Journalist. Founder and director of VilaWeb. Previously worked in media outlets such as El Temps, *TVE or* La Vanguardia, *mainly as a foreign affairs reporter. Partal was awarded the National Journalism Prize in 2004.*

When Catalonia becomes independent it will be at once both one of the oldest nations on the planet and one of the newest states. As a nation it will have to decide what role to play in the world and as a state it will have to adapt itself to the constantly changing conditions in contemporary international politics.

But what role should Catalonia play in the world? We are not, nor will we ever be—not even if some day we should unite with the rest of the Catalan Countries—a demographic, economic, or political superpower. We won't even be among the larger ones, among those that, based on macro-figures, are considered large by the world. But that doesn't matter. We simply have to recognize it, take it to heart, and then move on to construct our own path that makes us present in the world.

We will never be part of the group of big countries but we might easily make it into a group comprised of the good ones. The world today admires countries like Finland, the Netherlands, Iceland, Denmark, and New Zealand. These are solid societies, with a reasonable size and enough structure and flexibility to be able to offer their citizens the best state of well-being imaginable. Aspiring to be like Denmark or Finland but on the Mediterranean would be a goal that would make us one of the most attractive countries on Earth, without a need, I insist, to be one of the most powerful.

Joseph Nye, of Harvard University, wrote at the beginning of the century about the concept of "soft power", in contrast with "hard power", which is easy to deduce. Soft power consists of achieving respect and a certain stature based on constant seduction, rather than coercion.

It's easy to understand. If you close your eyes and think, for example, of the word *Brazil*, the most likely thing is that a smile will come to your face. It has soft power. The world recognizes that Brazil, besides being an economic, demographic, and cultural giant, is also a friendly, attractive country. If you think of the word *Iran*, on the other hand, it would be hard to smile, and rather more likely that a worried expression would result. Iran is respected out of fear but that is not positive. It is curious that for decades the United States has maintained a mix of soft and hard power by combining Hollywood and Silicon Valley with the aircraft carriers of Fort Bragg, to sum it up in just a few words.

Catalonia is a profoundly civic and civilized country. The fact that we haven't had our own state for 300 years has surely required us to be so. We are a country in which the major holiday consists of exchanging millions of books and flowers with one another, where the tradition has us build human towers in which we all support each other, and where the number one club of our most popular sport, the Futbol Club Barcelona, is recognized around the world as a team with ethical values and remarkable aesthetics.

If you go around the world and ask people what's the first thing they think of when you mention Catalonia, they answer that they associate our country with good soccer, but also with the art and architecture of Gaudí, Miró, and Picasso. And good cooking, such as the creativity of Ferran Adrià. Recently, there was a massive democratic march in Barcelona that surprised the world with its absolute lack of violence, and the happy faces amidst the largest economic crisis that Europe has ever seen.

It is unusual for anyone to associate us with hard power. We don't have an army or aggressive multinational corporations. And that is good and positive in the world in which we live.

To the list of soft power assets in Catalonia, we must add one more that is as obvious as it is crucial: the city of Barcelona. Barcelona is one of the most admired cities on the planet. It doesn't matter what those of us who live here every day think. Offer a contest on any website in the world where the prize is a trip to the favorite city of the winner and Barcelona will be on the list.

That is a huge advantage. In any part of the world, the question "What country is Catalonia?" has a ready answer in "the country of Barcelona!" Nowadays Barcelona is better known than Catalonia but it shares with Catalonia—it's not for nothing that it makes up half of the country—its values, and its image as a country. To take advantage of that is totally logical.

Barcelona is the gateway of Catalanness to the world. It is an indisputably cosmopolitan city but at the same time its most relevant essential character is its Catalanness. The global visibility of Barcelona brings with it a global visibility to Catalonia that without the capital would have to be made up with impossible investments. Barcelona lives off the Catalanness of the whole country but it also underscores the good and best of every part of the country. It's a symbiotic relationship, a sort of delta, rich and exuberant as they all are, in every sea in the world.

Encouraging and growing this soft power image of Barcelona and Catalonia is a project that fits well with our way of being and also with our interests. We won't have to be fake. We'll have enough by letting things fall into place as they really are.

In the process toward independence, the presence of an enormously plural and active community that has achieved great feats in other fields has been overwhelming obvious. An example of this is the process of holding the popular referendums.

Let's take a quick look at the referendum movement. There were seven rounds of referendums between 2009 and 2010. In total, there were polls in 518 of the 947 municipalities of Catalonia, including all of the important ones. Close to 900,000 citizens voted, which was more than 20 percent of the population. What is surprising is that this movement took place completely outside state organisms and support. Tens of thousands of volunteers literally built a state for a few hours; organizing an electoral process is one of the most difficult tasks that a state has. And they carried it out respecting the agreed-upon protocol, the international rules that validate any vote, and offering their fellow citizens the possibility of expressing themselves even though the state to which they belong denied it.

This amazing mobilization, 20 percent of the population participating in a self-organized process, makes it quite clear what sort of country we are. The reaction of the State was to prohibit the referendums and, in the first referendum that was held, to send the extreme right as a provocation. But that didn't get them anything. Indeed, the referendums were an act that evoked the memories of community building that was so valuable decades ago during the civil rights movement in the United States. It was an authentic empowering of the citizenry.

This is the kind of thing that Catalonia can bring to the world—the example and the model that can position us and be relevant. We are not a superpower. Except as a decent country.

How did we get here?

Cristina Perales-García

Ph.D. in Journalism and Communication Sciences from the Autonomous University of Barcelona (UAB) and professor of Communication at the University of Vic. Perales-García teaches Journalism and Audiovisual Communication. Her interests include the construction of identity markers by the media acting as political agents. She is a member of the UNESCOME research group (Unesco Chair for Intercultural Dialog throughout the Mediterranean) at the University of Rovira I Virgili (Tarragona) and of ComRess (Communication and Social Responsibility) of the Institute for Communication at UAB.

The Spanish Transition (1975–1978) did not answer the hopes of the sovereigntists in the various regions, such as Catalonia and the Basque Country, that demanded recognition of their differences. The urgency that was felt at the start of the transition toward democracy—in order to break with the legacy of dictatorship of 40 years of stagnation—and the belief in a single, unified Spain, have not been able to dampen the demands made currently by these nations within Spain, nations that have never been officially recognized as such by the central government or by the Spanish Constitution.

Discrepancies among some nationalists in the autonomous communities about how to define the State are the consequence of badly or unresolved conflicts with regard to the structure of the State and the definition of the collective identity of the autonomous communities, since in their very core, they are comprised of various groups whose differentiated identities have distinct levels of nationalization. There may also be divisions along ideological lines. The sum of these central conflicts has been settled by historic adversaries[1] in order to define the Catalan or Basque nationalist society and the controversial framework of political sovereignty.

Spanish uncertainty from 1975 on

The drafting of the Spanish Constitution aimed to give a legal answer to the political aspirations of the historic nationalities. In Article 2 of the Constitution, where the concept of Spain is explicitly defined—although not very clearly, if you take the text literaliy—the existence of peculiar situations is accepted. However, only one, indivisible nation is recognized:

> *"The Constitution is based on the indissoluble unity of the Spanish Nation, the common and indivisible homeland of all Spaniards; it recognizes and guarantees the right to self-government of the nationalities and regions of which it is composed and the solidarity among them all." (Article 2, Spanish Constitution, 1978)*

The ambiguity in the definition that determines the relationship between Spain and the so-called *nationalities* in the Spanish Constitution comes from trying to secure the widest support from the political parties, in order to get the text approved. It was the strategy that was chosen in order to make way for democracy, that arrived on shaky footing after 40 years of dictatorship.

1 In Zallo's opinion (1997), the historic subjects are social or political agents who attempt to manage their own destiny with respect to the conflict within the existing established order.

Nevertheless, three decades after the approval of the Spanish Constitution, political conflicts continue to exist that call into question the appropriateness of the current regional structure in Spain.

Creating a state of autonomies

The first government of the Spanish democracy formed in 1977 and, captained by Adolfo Suárez (UCD, moderate conservative party that gave way to the PP), took charge of the decentralization of the State administrative machinery, that is, to construct the State of Autonomies which first had to make it through a minimum amount of consensus in order to construct and approve a constitutional framework that allowed for such autonomies. It is in that moment that certain historical rights of the Basque, Catalan, and Galician territories began to be recognized. It was the first step toward the official development of the *nationalities*, a term that was picked up and formulated by the Spanish Constitution and that has since created so many misunderstandings. In this pre-autonomous context, the government saw the necessity of defining the territorial and political reality of Spain, that absolutely had to be contemplated in the future set of basic laws.

Once the Transition period was over, which culminated in the approval and enactment of the Spanish Constitution, elections were called. They were held on March 1, 1979, and UCD established itself as the political force with the most legitimacy to lead the democratic process. Nevertheless, Suárez resigned in January of 1981 after his party began to fall apart. The monarchy did not support him and he was succeeded by Leopoldo Calvo Sotelo.

The new political era begun with Calvo Sotelo revealed the weakness of the construction project of the State of Autonomies. After the attempted military coup in February 1981, which among other things served to signal that the democracy was still very fragile and that there were still sectors who were afraid of the "dismemberment of the fatherland", the president of the government attempted to redirect the autonomy question with the application of the *Harmonization of the Autonomous Process Law* (LOAPA). The objective of this law was to regulate the questions that relate to the territorial organization of the State that was in the process of being *reinvented*.

On July 31, 1981, the president of the government and the leader of the opposition, Felipe González, reflected the conclusions of the document in the first pacts on autonomies. Calvo Sotelo and González understood that it was necessary to undertake reforms that would unify the largest number of possible criteria on the territorial question. The Catalan and Basque autonomous aspirations served as a model for nationalist hopes that extended to other regions, and for this reason, the government deemed it necessary to create the law of harmonization. This law allowed the Spanish State to administer all of the autonomies in the same way and to smooth out the complaints that might arise from giving special treatment to the Basques and Catalans. It was later known as "coffee for all" and was widely criticized in the Basque Country and in Catalonia.

With the law of harmonization, Spain's map was redrawn to show 17 autonomies (with the same institutions, though with different competencies or areas of jurisdiction), and two autonomous cities: Ceuta and Melilla. The differences between the autonomous communities were ambiguously described in the law: five were considered "nationalities" (the Basque Country, Catalonia, Galicia, Andalusia, and Valencia), Navarre was considered a "chartered community", and the rest were "regions". On July 30, 1982, the Harmonization Law or LOAPA was approved.

From then onward, new autonomous agreements were established through which the statutes could be revised and modified with the objective of expanding the jurisdiction of those communities constituted between 1982 and 1983. Since then, there has been a whole process of deciding and arguing over which jurisdictions might be transferred between the State and the autonomous communities, which remains unresolved to this day.

It's precisely that element that the Basques and Catalans find democratically deficient. The historic territories, from LOAPA on, are treated as regions (disregarding the new vocabulary—*nationalities*—used in the Spanish Constitution). The Harmonization Law was more a subtraction of the autonomies' rights than any help toward territorial growth.

The Constitution and the Statutes of Autonomy

The constitutional pact meant, at the time, a recognition of the political particularity of the Basque Country, Catalonia, and Galicia, which were now to be called *nationalities*. The definition of democratic Spain was not at all clear, and in some aspects it was downright contradictory.

This fact can first be seen in the content of the Constitution with respect to the definition of Spain and the territories of which it is comprised. In Article 1.1 of the First Section, the Spanish Constitution defined Spain "as a social and democratic state, subject to the rule of law". The implication was that the citizens could participate in the exercising of political power and that they had full rights to do so: "National sovereignty belongs to the Spanish people, from whom all state powers emanate."

So, some territorial peculiarities were recognized, albeit with a high degree of imprecision. Only one nation was recognized, and that is Spain, and some territories were labeled with the new term, *nationality*, but not *nation*. At the same time and to some degree, it was suggested that they had a *national character*.

A heterogeneous state was acceptable ("it recognizes and guarantees the right to self-government" of the different parts of the State), although from a centralizing point of view ("the indissoluble unity of the Spanish Nation"). The Constitution was presented incomplete, with a representation of a state that was not yet completely outlined. The complete definition would have to include the subconstitutional government organs: the Statutes of Autonomy.

The Spanish Constitution of 1978 gave no satisfactory answer to the peripheral nationalism in the territorial organization of the State. After Franco's death, not all the nationalist movements responded in the same way to the development of the Transition. On the one hand, the moderate Catalan nationalists played an important role in conforming to the Spanish State, "demonstrating a high degree of politico-strategic pragmatism," in the words of Núñez Seixas (1999) and therefore delaying the demands for self-determination until after the consolidation of a firm and durable democratic system.

Following this premise, Catalanists opted to participate in the committee that edited the Spanish Constitution, and where formulas were discussed and for which there were nationalist demands that went unsatisfied. Nevertheless, the attitude of Catalan nationalism at that point was one of support for the Magna Carta, and they even campaigned for a yes vote when it was put to referendum, in which 67.91 percent of the electoral census and— of those a wide majority (90.46 percent)—voted in favor of the Spanish Constitution, according to the data published by the Official State Bulletin (BOE) on December 22, 1978.

But this attitude was not shared by the Basque Nationalists. The deficiencies in the Magna Carta were denounced from the start by both the Basque Nationalist Party (PNV) and the *abertzale* (Basque nationalist) left. The PNV did not join the Constitutional Committee, and it did not accept the text that came out of it because that text did not explicitly recognize the sovereignty of the Basque people. The PNV asked its voters to abstain. More than half of the Basque citizens who could vote followed their suggestion (51.6 percent).

Keeping in mind that 62.68 percent of the Basque citizenry voted either no (11.09 percent) or to abstain (51.6 percent), as the nationalist analysis makes clear, the constitutional text was not approved by the Basques. This fact is often used to question the legitimacy of the Spanish Constitution in the Basque Country and to note that they don't identify with what the Constitution proposes.

The lack of consensus and the impossibility of building a definition of Spain in which the nations within the Spanish State are recognized is a struggle that continues to contribute to various kinds of negotiation strategies: a demand for a higher level of control by the Basque and Catalan communities and, recently in Catalonia, the full rethinking of the budget system with respect to Spain, which has been denied by the central government without them offering any alternative to the Catalan demand. Now, after more than 30 years of attempts to resolve a question of definition, the Government of Catalonia, at the request of the citizen mobilization, has opened a new political legislature marked by the definition of the process of transition toward independence, a process that outlines the political transition toward the recognition of the Catalan nation. The first decade of the 21st century has been characterized in Spain by attempts at sovereignty by some of the "historic territories" that make up the State. The aspirations for more self-government and even independence—as the Government of Catalonia has positioned itself since September—have been rejected by both Socialist and conservative governments that have held the helm of the central government, to the point that they refuse to allow an open debate that might facilitate the smoothing of tensions between the center and the periphery.

On the one hand, in 2006 Catalonia approved a new Statute that aimed to substitute the previous one, which had been in place since 1979. Even though Catalonia has based its laws on this new Statute since 2006, Spain's Constitutional Court agreed to hear an appeal of unconstitutionality[2] brought by the conservative, neoliberal People's Party in the Congress of deputies. The Court ruling,[3] issued four years later, on June 28, 2010, said that Catalonia's self-proclamation as a nation had no juridical standing and ruled a further 14 articles inconstitutional.

---

2 The following link has details on the basis of the appeal of unconstitutionality: http://www10.gencat.net/eapc_revistadret/recursos_interes/especial%20estatut/documents%20especial%20estatut/SDJR/recursos/4_a_1_recurs_pp/ca

3 You can read the details of the ruling in Spain's "Official State Bulletin", the BOE, (in Spanish).

The reaction in Catalonia was of general outrage. On July 10, more than a million people marched in protest against the Constitutional Court's ruling, organized by cultural groups like Òmnium Cultural[4]. The lemma at the head of the demonstration read: *We are a nation. We decide.*[5] Between 2009 and April of 2011, 554 towns and cities—out of a total of 947—organized popular referendums on independence. Nearly 900,000 votes were cast: 18.8 percent of the citizens called to vote participated. Votes in favor of self-determination were a overwhelming majority—92.2 percent—and negative votes garnered just 6 percent[6]. These popular referendums were largely symbolic. Neither the Catalan government at the time nor the central government in Madrid ever recognized the validity of these grassroots organized referendums.

---

4 http://www.omnium.cat/www/omnium/en/history.html.

5 See the detailed analysis on the press coverage by State, Basque, and Catalan media during the July 10th demonstration as a consequence of the Court ruling in Perales, Xambó and Xicoy (2012).

6 Data thanks to the Coordinador Nacional de les Consultes, published: http://www.coordinadoranacional.cat/municipis/resultats/.

Judo in Madrid

Alfred Bosch

Writer and historian, MP and leader of ERC (Catalan pro-independence Republican left) in Spanish Congress

Recently I held a debate with an official from the ruling party in (autonomous) Catalonia. I was insisting about the importance of working in Madrid and furthering our pro-independence cause in the capital of Spain. He was a staunch Catalan patriot, and sustained that he wanted separation as much as me, or even more; indeed, he believed that doing anything in Madrid was pure nonsense. I remarked that Artur Mas, his party boss and president of (autonomous) Catalonia, had just made two historical announcements in Madrid; these statements had revolutionized Catalan politics and triggered international attention. He fell dead silent.

As in any process of national liberation, we encounter voices calling for a complete withdrawal from the seat of power. Some people will have nothing to do or nothing to hear from the capital—where institutions and forces have punished Catalonia for ages. Many others would not be so adamant but would simply find it absurd and tedious to take the trouble to travel 625km and back just to try useless dealings with Madrid, as if forgetting the fact that we are not yet independent. Similar criticism was encountered by those who headed for their respective metropolitan capitals in times of national liberation elsewhere: Gandhi from India, Purnell from Ireland, Martí from Cuba, Nkrumah from Ghana ... and many of our predecessors from Catalonia as well.

Let me say that Madrid is portrayed here as a political reality rather than a big bunch of ordinary citizens busily looking for a normal life. Madrid is where the Spanish government sits. The legislative chambers are there, as well as the Crown, the ministries, the army headquarters, the embassies, and increasingly so, transnational companies and broadcasters, which tend to drift under the shade of power. Madrid is, therefore, also a concept and has to be understood as a weighty political factor, like Brussels or Washington DC.

No one would be foolish enough to think that Catalan independence has to be gained solely in Madrid, but no one would be blind enough to ignore that it has to be gained from Madrid. Especially if the desired process is a democratic and peaceful one—as is the case—it has to be built and nourished within the Catalan bounds. But that does not imply that the seat of power has to be skipped; it must be visited, studied, utilized, and ultimately envisaged as the location for negotiating a friendly divorce. That is the reason President Artur Mas staged his epic declarations in Madrid, vindicating plebiscitary elections and self-determination. No other political theatre or loudspeaker can be compared to those of the capital city.

There are three outstanding obstacles in the way of free determination for Catalonia, and they have to be dealt with in Madrid. The three of them derive from age-long stigmas of Spanish power, and need to be confronted.

The first barrier could be defined as *democratic shortage*. The Kingdom of Spain is a very young parliamentary democracy, with less than forty years of ballot tradition compared to a long legacy of bullet tradition. The army is still a warrant of territorial unity, the monarchy heads the military structure, the king is legally unaccountable and unchallengeable, minorities have few safeguards, and the bipartisan pattern of Spanish politics often leaves Catalans starving in the political wild, left out of parliamentary dynamics. Catalan parties are underrepresented in the Spanish system of constituencies, in Congress, and even more in the Senate.

Democratic malfunctioning leads to huge frustration, as was the case of the 2006 Statute of Autonomy of Catalonia. This text was approved in (the Catalan autonomous) parliament and voted in the polls, just to be cut down by the Spanish legislative and eventually blown up by the highly politicized Spanish Constitutional Court. The further away you drive from Madrid, the more this democratic shortage affects voters. That Catalonia was a hotbed of anarchism in the early 20th century was not a mere coincidence; mistrust regarding Spanish authorities had a lot to do with it, and right now such mistrust is still a driving force behind separatism.

One of the main functions of Catalan politicians in Madrid, thus, is the patient, stubborn denunciation of undemocratic practices. From a reformist point of view, such a job is clearly exasperating and futile; but for champions of independence it can be a blessing in disguise. The realization that Spanish power is anti-democratic heightens the need to break with an unbendable system, it dissipates hopes of changing Spanish power into a kinder, milder reality and therefore pushes minds and hearts toward rupture. It is not strange to meet inhabitants of Madrid who confess the urge to exit the Kingdom … although not knowing where to go from there. Catalans are very much aware that leaving the Kingdom is a sound option.

The second obstacle could be defined as *legal blockade*. The argument that something is not legal, or even illegal, is endlessly exploited by Spanish advocates of the status quo. It has been sustained against any measure of devolution to Catalans, be it economic, political, or cultural. It is in fact the main stumbling block upheld against self-determination or independence. It is not much of an argument, since nothing is legal until it is enacted, and Catalan independence has obviously not been enacted, for if it had, no one would demand it any more. Looking back at world history, few if any paths toward independence have been in accordance with established legal procedures; such political prospects are seldom enshrined in constitutional provisions.

It is true that the Spanish Constitution of 1978 considers Spain a unitary state and the monarchy and the army are the gatekeepers of its territorial integrity. It is also true that this piece of legislation was drafted under the still-beating legacy of the Franco military dictatorship: that time has since passed; that some forceful clauses have been altogether disregarded (such as military service); that new clauses have been rushed in by express methods (like the deficit limitations introduced in 2011); and that, naturally, all legal texts ought to be prone to amendments.

Regardless of these commonsense considerations, the Constitution and other major Spanish laws have been presented as a conservative cage designed to prevent change rather than build a house of liberties. Any proposal for increased self-government has always met a vicious circle; the law is the law, and it must be abided. New developments are not possible because they are not legal, and if they are not legal they cannot be developed. This has been repeated hundreds of time in Spanish congress, ignoring the obvious fact: that MPs are not robocops, but legislators elected to set new rules and adapt them to evolving times and troubles. The function of legislators is precisely to engineer useful laws, trying to respond to the people's demands.

The same day that the UK government delegated in the Scottish autonomous government the power of holding a referendum for independence, our party (ERC) proposed exactly the same method for holding an identical poll. The proposal was defeated on the grounds that it was not legal, when there is a specific article in the Spanish Constitution that allows such a delegation, and it has been used in the past for devolving, for instance, police capacity to the Catalan administration. Other similar and imaginative resources have been suggested, and the reply has always been the same: nonlegal devices cannot be accepted. The vicious circle is shut and there is no predictable majority for opening it.

The situation can only be defeated by engaging in two alternative paths: international law and (new) Catalan legislation. Global treaties and charters accept self-determination and the rule of democratic mandates, two principles that all Catalan pro-independence parties or movements embrace at heart. There is, therefore, an option that would enable us to break the aforementioned vicious circle: drafting specific Catalan norms for holding a poll on independence and appealing, in parallel, to international mediation.

The third hurdle I would like to mention is *economic stranglehold*. For decades, and some would even say for centuries, the Spanish government has lived partly on Catalan wealth. Being the powerhouse of Spain, and with a sturdy productive economy, Catalonia has paid a disproportionate share of Spanish bills. In the last 30 years, about 50 percent of Catalan taxes have never returned as services or social benefits; more than double the amount delivered by the EU to Spain in various development funds. With a population of 16 percent, today Catalans account for 24 percent of revenues. This has been tolerated with compliance in times of fortune, but in years of crisis the burden has proven unbearable and has generated quite a temper—anger, in fact. The general feeling is that Catalans are being plundered by Madrid, and that this constant pillage chokes the economy.

Many different solutions have been offered. The most obvious is Catalonia using the fiscal arrangement that is in place for the Basque Country and Navarre, known as *economic concert* (by means of a fiscal pact), and which implies fiscal sovereignty: that is, collecting taxes and then negotiating the share that Madrid takes. This, however, has not been accepted by the Spanish government and most surely never will, as it would stop a major flow of taxes into depleted Spanish coffers. Other attempted deals have turned sour in the short run, clashing against a stubborn reality; Madrid will not devolve tax control to the Catalan administration.

Many experts believe this is the main obstacle for Catalan independence or for higher levels of home rule. Spain simply cannot drop its main source of cash, and will fight tooth and nail to preserve it. However, even if we ignore the unfair and undemocratic nature of such reasoning, we have to admit likewise that this stranglehold is also the main driving force behind the urge for independence, as it turns a matter of national spirit into a matter of life and death. It is true that Spanish power will make a fierce stand against the interruption of Catalan funding. It is also true that the leap into independence would be extremely risky for a Catalonia with no tax collectors, no cash, no credit, and no loans in the international market. However, we must concede as well that prospects are gloomier by the day, and that survival points more and more, every passing hour, to economic liberation.

All in all, the Madrid factor must be seen as crucial in blocking further devolution, and as a serious obstacle in the way of an orderly, civilized, bilateral, and constitutional trip toward free determination. The Kingdom of Spain is not the United Kingdom, however similar Catalonia might be to Caledonia. So a British solution seems very unlikely, and apparently this diminishes hope in the minds of many freedom-loving Catalans. The awareness that Madrid is ready to use all its strength in pushing back the popular will could possibly discourage efforts toward a decent settlement. Any advance by Catalan grass-roots society or Catalan administration would look doomed to a prospect of trouble and even sufferance ahead.

On the other hand, sheer force can generate positive reactions. It can lead to intelligent and imaginative devices and help to further the cause. As in Judo tactics, the ruthless energy of the opponent can be exploited against him. Perhaps the best example of this skill was shown in the popular referenda of 2009–2011, when ordinary citizens organized polls on independence in the majority of Catalan municipalities, including Barcelona. The movement was a big success; close to 1 million votes were cast, more than 90 percent in favor of independence, and something that was up to then impossible became possible. The Spanish State proved helpless to prevent it. The stronger judoka was tripped by the smaller one, falling in full fury flat on its face.

Catalan pro-independence feeling was not among the most relevant in late 20th century Europe. At the start of the second decade of the 21st, it is clearly the most outstanding in the continent. This evolution owes much to the brutish attitude of Madrid and the clever reaction of Catalans, who opposed a democratic shortage with an extra dose of democracy; who dealt with a legal blockade by availing themselves of international principles and uncovering legal alternatives; and who confronted an economic stranglehold by demanding full sovereignty. The Madrid factor probably explains a lot about the progress of pro-independence mood and the conversion of a relatively harmless linguistic and cultural claim into a mighty democratic, ethical, and economic mass movement. It is always useful to have a clear villain in opposition; and if such rival is a consummate Goliath, there will be no lack of determination or aim on the side of David.

European patriots

Muriel Casals

Ph.D. in Economics. Professor and former vice dean of International Relations (2002–2005) at the Autonomous University of Barcelona. Casals has worked and published on Industrial Reconversions, particularly in the textile sector. She has taught economics and collaborated in various media, including El Temps *magazine and Catalunya Ràdio. She was one of the "Top Thinkers" in the FT publication* European Union, the next fifty years *in 2007. Currently, she is the president of Òmnium Cultural, an organization with 32,000 members that has worked in favor of the Catalan language and culture for 51 years.*

"Because of their spiritual character, the cultural sector is the one that has best been able to maintain Catalan meaning in the works they've created." These words form part of the report presented by the Minister of Culture Carles Pi i Sunyer to the Parliament of Catalonia at the end of 1938, in the midst of the Civil War.

There are other phrases in that same report that may hold interest for us right now, like when he notes the importance of "the unified efforts of all those who feel, intervene in, or work for our culture" or when he says that it's important to respect "the spontaneity of the initiative and the effort of each of the individuals, groups, and organizations that collaborate". "More than the work of the Department, it's like the cultural manifestation of the *Spirit of Catalonia*," he concludes.

Why am I recalling the role of the Minister of Culture from the war years? Because he expresses the desire of putting culture in the center of Catalan politics, even in times of extreme hardship. It's obvious that in 1938 there were urgent matters that directly affected the life of the citizenry but those urgent matters and immediate survival needs (which was strictly the case then) don't mean that we must ever give up what makes us human, which is culture.

When Òmnium Cultural was created in 1961, the circumstances were not nearly as dramatic as in 1938, but they were extremely difficult. The struggle continued against the victors of the war who were enemies of Catalan culture as surely as they were enemies of culture in general. In that moment, defending language and culture was the obvious way of defending the country.

The initial task of Òmnium Cultural, its foundational objective, was to give Catalan language classes. The idea was to teach people to read and write in the very same language that the fascist regime had prohibited in schools. In the 1960s things had begun to loosen up. There were signals on the horizon. The first books began to appear in Catalan again, and the phenomenon of the "Catalan New Song" had begun. People began to feel hope at returning to normalcy, that is, being able to live in Catalan.

If democracy returned, the first thing we'd need would be teachers who were able to teach in Catalan. For too many years it had been impossible to get such training, so Òmnium took on the responsibility of providing this service, with many limitations but with decision and a fair number of volunteers. Rigorous classes were given, tests were administered, and diplomas were awarded, all of which would have corresponded to the Catalan public administration that we didn't have. It was definitely a supplemental task.

Today, we are lucky enough to live in a peaceful, democratic society. The material difficulties that we have to face come from the bad economic times in which we find ourselves and which, in the Catalan case, are exacerbated by the fact that we don't control our own tax revenues.

Òmnium Cultural believes that our culture and the people who work in the cultural sector need special attention and support. We know that Catalans nowadays, whoever they are and wherever they're from, are deciding what our culture will be like in the short term. We live this moment as a challenge to our intelligence, creativity, and will, and are confident that it will help us grow as a country. We are proud to realize that today, with such a diverse population, we Catalans can offer a wide variety of contributions that enrich our shared culture.

We also know that the responsibility of the future of the Catalan language and culture belongs to us, the citizens of Catalonia. After the longest period of autonomous Catalan government within a democratic Spain, we have come to realize that if we stay within the Spanish State, our future as a people, with the particular characteristics that define us, is in grave danger. The Spanish governments have clearly and explicitly demonstrated their wish to assimilate us into their culture, and we know without any doubt that there is no place in Spain for diversity.

The future is in our hands. It's for that reason that Òmnium, a cultural organization, dedicates an important part of its energy and resources toward working for the construction of a future Catalan State. We need a political power with no more limitations than those derived from the transfer of sovereignty to the European Union. It is precisely the fact of belonging to a group in which many decisions are made which makes the process of secession that much less dramatic. We are constructing a wider group that will be a new united Europe and we are confident of the value of what we bring to the table.

Now that we Catalans have demonstrated our desire for political power, we must also recognize how urgent it is to exercise the clearest expression of this power: the ability to manage our own budget. At this moment, the Catalan government cannot apply its own policies, whether they be cultural or of any other type, because of the financial strangulation to which it is subjected by the Spanish government. In this context, it is not surprising that a cultural organization has among its principal objectives the management of our own tax revenue and that it propose as an urgent necessity that a significant part of the income that comes from the productive efforts of Catalans be collected by an agency that we feel belongs to the Catalan people, and that we can control.

We defend Catalonia as a new state in Europe out of Catalan patriotism and out of European patriotism. We hope to be able to add our Catalan cultural and linguistic contributions to increase the richness and diversity of the continent that we share with our European compatriots.

The battle for the audience

Ignasi Aragay

Journalist, deputy director of the daily ARA. *Expert in Cultural journalism. Author of the books,* Diccionari Montaigne [A dictionary of Montaigne], El lector obsedit [The obsessed reader], Anolecrab, *which, read backwards, is Barcelona], and* Què pensa Salvador Cardús [What Salvador Cardús thinks].
Married with three children.

Catalan is a language with 1,000 years of history. Currently there are 9 million potential speakers, most of whom live within the confines of the Spanish State, in the regions of Catalonia, the Balearic Islands, and the Valencian Country. Like French, Spanish, or Italian, it is a Romance language that evolved from Latin after the break up of the Roman Empire. Its golden era was during the 14th and 15th centuries when Catalonia was an independent country and a Mediterranean maritime power. Despite the political and intellectual decline of the following centuries, despite the constant prohibitions and persecutions of the Spanish monarchy, Catalan has always been the language of the people and has never stopped being written or printed. At the end of the 19th century, with the push of the industrial revolution at home, the emergence of mass communication media, and the slow political and cultural recovery—which gave rise to figures such as the architect Antoni Gaudí—Catalonia's language has won an ever increasingly central place in society, always in competition with, and at a disadvantage to Spanish.

Despite two brutal dictatorships and despite a genocidal civil war, the 20th century has been a golden century for Catalan literature especially in the fields of poetry and the novel. It was a period with highs and lows for the Catalan media, with moments of great creativity and widespread reach—like in the 1930s during the Spanish Republic and the Catalan autonomous government, or like the present—and moments of ostracism, like during the aforementioned dictatorships, especially that of General Franco (1939–1975).

Today, Catalan and Spanish are co-official languages in Catalonia, the Balearic Islands, and in the Valencian Country, although it is only in Catalonia that Catalan has had the benefit of an effective and continuous promotion campaign over the last 35 years, both within the school system (though the Spanish government is currently trying to eliminate Catalan's status as the language of instruction in the education system) as well as in communications and politics. In other areas, like cinema, the judiciary system, or in business, Catalan's presence is reduced. The society has deep-rooted diglossic behaviors, that is, it is particular about which language to use in which context or with which interlocutors. Catalonia, with 7.5 million inhabitants—of which 42 percent consider Catalan their primary, habitual language and more than 90 percent understand it—has at its disposal a set of media outlets that use both languages, in which, since the end of Franco's dictatorship, Catalan has slowly gained ground, although at a disadvantage.

Despite some outlying examples, until the public Catalan TV channel (TV3) started transmitting regularly in 1984, one could not really speak of general Catalan television, with a variety of programming, including fiction, news, and entertainment shows. The years of splendor for this channel were the ones that preceded the opening of Spain to the private television companies. Until that point, TV3 had a steady audience share of 30 percent and it revolutionized and modernized its contents and style, in the context of a very limited and old-fashioned television ecosystem. During the 90s, TV3 was able to maintain audience share between 25 and 30 percent. After the appearance of digital terrestrial television (DTT), the reach of Catalan public television, despite having additional channels to offer, and despite fighting for leadership within Catalonia, fell to its current audience share of 19.3 percent in 2011, where, one must note, it remains in first place. The increasing fragmentation of both the offerings and the audience, as well as the budget cuts affecting spending on public television due to the prevailing austerity policies in the European Union, have reduced the number of channels in the Catalan Television conglomerate, and foreshadow a further loss of share during the next few years. This loss in the linguistic terrain will not be compensated by the appearance of private channels in Catalan, which have yet to make much of a mark (2.7 percent share for 8TV in 2011).

All of the percentages mentioned up to this point refer strictly to the area of Catalonia, since the transmissions of the Catalan public television in the Balearics and in Valencia has always been prohibited by Spanish legislation, and only sometimes circumvented in extralegal fashion by concerned citizens. Currently, Catalan TV does not reach these areas, nor do transmissions from those areas reach Catalonia. Meanwhile, the Valencian and Balearic public television channels, created in 1989 (Canal9) and in 2005 (IB3) respectively, are being radically cut back due to the economic crisis and decatalanized by their respective governments, both of which are in hands of the Spanish nationalist right (Partit Popular). Before the recent cuts to the workforce, Canal9 had about 10 percent share in its territory and IB3 had about 7.5 percent.

Beyond the numbers, public television in Catalan has been an extremely important force in the struggle to normalize the language among the greater public and to strengthen the cultural imagination with its own star system, besides being a pillar of the international-tending audiovisual industry centered in Barcelona. In Catalonia, in addition, the clear leadership position achieved by the news programs—including nightly news, debates, and magazines—has also played a crucial role in informing public opinion, which is more and more distanced from Spanish public opinion.

In this respect, the existence of a unique Catalan press, completely differentiated from that of Madrid, the market leader in Spain, is particularly relevant. The Catalan newspaper reader buys very few papers based in the kingdom's capital, and at the same time, reads increasingly more in Catalan. The newspapers that are leaders in the market are, according to average figures for 2011, the veteran, conservative *La Vanguardia*—with a daily run of 175,000 print copies—and the progressive and populist *El Periódico*—with 104,000 copies. Both are published in two editions, that is they publish one version in Spanish and a translated version in Catalan. In the case of *La Vanguardia*, sales of the two editions are split almost evenly—the Catalan version began publication in 2011—while the proportion of Spanish to Catalan (begun in 1997) of *El Periódico* is about 60/40. *El Periódico* has digital editions in both languages, while *La Vanguardia* has a robust digital edition in Spanish and only a digital copy of the print edition in Catalan.

Continuing with data from 2011, the leading paper in Spain, *El País*, is a distant third and leans progressive, but only sells 38,500 copies a day in Catalonia. Next come two Catalan-only papers, the historic and conservative *El Punt-Avui*—30,000 print copies sold—and the two-year-old *Ara*, which is progressive and Catalanist, and sells 15,000 print copies daily but has 1.5 million monthly unique visitors to its digital edition, where it is an active leader in Catalan. In Catalonia, the local press also plays an important role, either in Catalan or in bilingual editions.

Apart from *El País*, the rest of the important Spanish dailies—*El Mundo*, *ABC*, and *La Razón*—all with ultraconservative tendencies, have a very slight impact in Catalonia, where they are perceived as hostile press given their constant attacks on the language and the very institutions of the Catalan government. They also have a historical editorial trend that has been accentuated by the current pro-independence movement taking place in Catalan society and politics. On November 25, 2012, the movement culminated in the election of a regional Parliament in which two thirds are in favor of convoking a referendum on self-determination.

The newspaper market is territorially fragmented where Catalan is spoken. *La Vanguardia* and *El Periódico* make it to the Balearics and to the Valencian Country, but paradoxically only their Spanish editions are sent and they are not big sellers. The only Catalan newspaper that is sold throughout the Catalan linguistic territory is *Ara*, but in a limited way, especially in Valencia. In the Balearics and in Valencia, the most popular selling papers are the regional ones in Spanish, followed by the Madrid-based papers.

It's in radio where the Catalan language has achieved an important penetration in Catalonia in the last few years, doubling its audience share in the last decade (2002–2012) with the two Catalan language stations at the top of the ranking, relegating the Spanish group SER (430,000 monthly listeners) to third place. Currently, the most listened to radio is the private RAC1, which belongs to the Godó Group (which also owns *La Vanguardia* and 8TV). Established in 2000, RAC1 reached 700,000 monthly listeners in 2012, followed by the public station, Catalunya Ràdio, with 600,000 listeners.

If we take communications in its broad sense, it's also important to underscore that Catalonia is the capital of book publishing, obviously in Catalan, but also in Spanish, competing with Madrid. The roots of large publishing houses like Planeta, Bertelsmann, and RBA, and a wide variety of medium and smaller specialized houses is the product of continuous activity, which has spread to Spain, Latin America, and the rest of the world. Publishing is suffering its own particular business crisis at the hands of emerging technologies at the same time that it is being buffeted by the global and also specifically Spanish financial crisis, and it's safe to say that it's not having an easy time of it.

In summary, Catalan media has a long history and despite the difficulties of the financial crisis, shows remarkable dynamism that will respond to three factors. First, to the vitality and cultural diversity of a society that is always open to changes but also proud of its traditions. Second, to the political battle in national terms between a Catalonia that aspires to create an independent state and a Spain that looks to deny that possibility. And third, to the competition between languages.

With respect to this last point, it's important to remember that in addition to Catalan and Spanish, as a destination spot for tourists and as a net importer of immigrants—there were 1.5 million new residents between 1990 and 2000—there is a very diverse population in Catalonia, with more than 300 maternal languages that come from North Africa, Asia, Latin America, Eastern Europe, and English-speaking countries, a diversity that already has its own media channels, as in the case of the *Dayly Dost*, a Pakistani community paper and the *Latino*.

Strangers in our own land

Germà Bel

Professor of Economics at the University of Barcelona. Visiting professor at Cornell University and Princeton University in 2012–2013. Bel's main interest is the interaction between governments and markets, and his research focuses on the economics and politics of public sector reform. His latest books are Infrastructure and the Political Economy of Nation Building in Spain *(1720/2010) (Sussex Academic Press, 2012; published previously in Spanish and Catalan as* Espanya, capital Paris*), and* The Economics and Politics of High-Speed Rail: Lessons from Experiences Abroad *(Lexington Books, with Daniel Albalate).*

In Catalonia, there is a portion of the population that has always believed that creating a sovereign state is a priority. A very relevant fact of the past few years is that a new part of the population has signed up for this objective, even though it wasn't traditionally their preferred model. About these, we could say that they are in favor of the creation of a sovereign state as a second choice, because their first choice, their ideal—which was reforming Spain so that Catalonia and the Catalans with their own national identity could fit better—has turned out to be impossible.

Spain has spent the last 300 years emulating French principles of nation-building; that is, the construction of a compact, egalitarian nation without differences among individuals and their territories. Difference is seen as a measure of inequality (under a concept of eminently formal, but not substantive inequality). The existence of a variety of national identities within Spain has always been a thorn in the side of this project of uniformity, a project that has been expressed in economic terrain, or in public, cultural, and linguistic policies.

As I have said, however, the notion of egalitarianism is formal, but not substantive. Actually, it is totally the opposite, as has been documented in many areas. A few examples follow.

In the area of public financing, one often hears the mantra "it is the individuals who pay, not the regions". That is partially true, and partially not. There could be, and in fact, there are, important territorial differences in the intensity of repression of fraud, in the proportion of activities that are carried out "under the table" and so on. But, what is indisputable is that spending is done by territory in Spain, in the European Union, and in any other political organization. And in that respect, the well documented lack of equality between the Mediterranean territories and the rest is stubbornly persistent.[1] It's not a coincidence that the three Spanish regions that have the highest fiscal deficits with the State are precisely the Balearic Islands, Catalonia, and the Valencian Country. That is true despite the fact that other, wealthier regions don't contribute to redistribution and that, the Valencian Country is in fact poorer that the Spanish average.

---

1 IEF. 2008. Las balanzas fiscales de las CC AA españolas con las AA. públicas centrales 2005. Madrid: Instituto de Estudios Fiscales, http://www.ief.es/Investigacion/Temas/BalanzasFiscales_Publicacion_BF_15_07_08_vf.pdf Bel 2012a).

Bel, Germà. 2012a. "De paganos ricos y pobres, y de algunospolizones." La Vanguardia, 2.11.2012 (http://www.ub.edu/graap/NP_BEL2412.2.pdf)

The policies for deciding how to allocate infrastructure resources in Spain has been and continues to be obsessively radial. Instead of following transportation priorities, it follows political priorities with the clear aim of subordinating one city to another. The political capital has the upper hand, and the rest of the network is at its service.[2] This can be illustrated (but not justified) for example, by the fact that there are sections of railway with little or no transit that are already or about to be served by high-speed trains to and from Madrid, while in Tarragona, 100km south of Barcelona—the busiest land corridor in the south of Europe—there are still 35km of single direction rail that must handle the entire load.

The infrastructure policy in Spain is characterized by its inefficiency, a postponement of works on the periphery, and also by a blatant lack of equality that is made obvious when one looks at how Spanish highway tolls are paid. In the central plateau and in the radial network that converges on Madrid, payment is made fundamentally with State budget money. On the periphery, and especially in the Mediterranean and the Valley of the Ebre (and also the Galician coast), it is the user who pays.[3] This asymmetry is over 20 years old, and when I have had the opportunity to discuss it in meetings with the State power brokers, the response has always been, more or less, that it's normal that richer territories should pay and that the poorer ones should not, completely ignoring the fact that Madrid is the richest city and region and the few tollbooths that remain there have recently been rescued by the general budget.

From my point of view, this breaches the principle of equality that—in whatever government—must be applied equally to all of the individuals and territories in the Polis or political community. When different policies of equality are instituted in different territories of a single state, we don't have a unified political state, we are faced with a structure of colonial exploitation, where the different territories are not interchangeable, and therefore, a single criteria of equality can be omitted (again, by whoever is in power) in the rest of the territory under the control of the state.

The *summum* or maximum exaggeration of this breach of equality in Spain occurs in the cultural and linguistic areas. Based on an ideological principle (which is completely distinct from basic principles of philology)

---

2 Bel, Germà. 2010. *Espana, capital Paris*. Barcelona: Destino (Catalan Edition, La Campana 2011) English edition: *Infrastructure and the Political Economy of Nation Building in Spain, 1720–2010*. Sussex Academic Press.

3 Ibid.

that Spanish is the "common language" of all of the citizens of the Spanish State, the idea is to institute a rule of "egalitarian treatment for all Spaniards", which is translated into the principle of the freedom to choose the language of instruction at school, as long as you choose Spanish. This is justified with the fiction that Spanish is everyone's language, as I mentioned earlier. What is hidden (again) is the lack of equality: citizens whose mother tongue is something besides Spanish cannot choose the language of instruction at school because—they tell us—Spanish is always available and "that is also our language". It is also in this area that culture is treated with a colonial point of view. The metropolis' "common" language is protected, they say, while the language of the colonies, the "special one" is not.

Once again, there is no thought of observing the minimum requirements of equality of rights or obligations of all of the citizens of the State, which does not behave like an integrated and inclusive Polis but rather an opportunity for some national identities to dominate others. Let them ask—if they claim that is not the case—the tens of thousands of Valencian families who are not offered the choice of Valencian [Catalan] as the language of instruction, and the rights of whom are perfectly invisible to the Spanish education authorities.

At the end of the day, the questions related to culture and language are the ones most illustrative of the differences. From here stems the obsession with uniformity. The only indisputable fact, however, is that in Catalonia, Spanish is a required language (according to Article 3 of the Constitution) and Catalan is not. Maybe no language should be required. But, the current situation, in which the language of another country is required in my country while my own language is not required in my country infringes every notion of egalitarian principles. The State imposes norms and rules that make one feel like a stranger in one's own land.

Let's go back to the beginning. I believe that an important segment of the population, among which I count myself, have tried to change the rules and the way of organizing Spain as a state to help it transition from its hegemonic Castilian character and worldview into an inclusive country that beyond respecting plurality, would actually promote it and take advantage of its richness. But, that has turned out to be an impossible mission, for various reasons, primarily because a very large majority of the citizens of Castilian Spain are perfectly happy with a nation cast in the French mold. One must recognize that flexibility and plurality bring uncertainty and that many people prefer the certainty and security that are offered by centralization, rigidity, and uniformity, which offer a less complex world, though one also condemned to lag in the past.

This is the dilemma that is now facing many Catalans who, even as they avoid choosing polarizing, extreme solutions to the problem of Catalonia's relationship with Spain, see ever more clearly that, when all is said and done, only two options remain: 1) uniformity and certainty, that is, assimilation, or 2) complexity, entrepreneurship, and assumption of risks, that is, our own state.

At the end of the day, one of the most important factors in the social and politic dynamic of Catalonia since the end of the 1990s is that many Catalans now feel like strangers in their own country thanks to the actions of the unitary and exclusive State. It is for that reason, that in the end we have to choose between changing states or changing countries. From what we're seeing, it seems like there are many more of us who would prefer to change states rather than bury our own country.

Yet another wiki?

Àlex Hinojo

GLAM (Galleries, Libraries, Archives, and Museums) Ambassador in Barcelona. Wikipedian since 2007 and recipient of a Museum Studies degree with honors, Hinojo is responsible for piloting a full network of successful museum-Wikipedia projects and outreach events, like being the first Wikipedian in Residence at Museu Picasso. Today he serves as Open Knowledge consultant for several museums, including the Fundació Joan Miró, the Museu Picasso, and the Dalí Theatre-Museum. His research focuses on the power of technology and open knowledge as a way to improve accessibility to museum collections and reach wider audiences, and he's especially interested in multilingual translation projects.

Did you know that Viquipèdia—the Catalan version of Wikipedia—was just the second version of this encyclopedia to have articles, right after the English-language version and weeks before versions began to appear in other languages that are much more widely spoken throughout the world?

The Catalan Wikipedia is just one example of Catalans on the internet and of their civic activism in favor of their language. With more than 400,000 articles, it's the 15th biggest Wikipedia in a ranking by number of articles. If you take into account the number of Catalan speakers—about 11.5 million[1]—it should be in 80th or 90th place. And it's not just the number of articles, Viquipèdia is also a leader in quality: it dominates the ranking of the 1,000 articles that every Wikipedia should have, even outranking the all-powerful English edition. Those who write in Catalan on the internet still have a decidedly activist character borne of the prevailing diglossia. Even still, the position of the Catalan language is not fully normalized, despite its advances. Therefore, the editors of the Catalan Wikipedia stand out for their hard-working attitudes, their desire to do more, and be better than the others. It's a reflection of the Catalan character: our only weapon to gain the world's confidence has always been our work ethic.

On the internet, net neutrality and the existence of open platforms that are easily adaptable to different languages have been key factors in the success of networked Catalan successes. The net favors activism and facilitates getting people with similar interests together: it is a tool that connects. In a society with a tradition of community involvement like Catalonia, the net has been ideal for making our language and culture visible. Without political borders or obstacles, we are able to grow more than we can in the real world, which is significant given the numerous roadblocks that we suffer there. In the latest poll taken of readers and editors on Viquipèdia, in January 2012, the principal reasons that editors gave for explaining why they had begun to work on Wikipedia were to facilitate the free access of information, help others, and share the Catalan linguistic patrimony.

Even though it is horizontal and neutral, the internet tends to reproduce the models we have in the physical world. When local associations, chapters, or divisions are organized from whatever international group or project, it's often by country. Since Catalans always want to be there with our own voice, we defend groups that are defined by interest instead of by political borders. Our particular situation as a nation without a state has often been the catalyst

1 http://www.antaviana.cat/bloc/wp-content/uploads/2012/03/catalan-on-the-internet.html

that has generated changes in a variety of international organizations. One example of this is the .cat domain, which was the very first top-level domain to be awarded to a linguistic and cultural community—and not to a state—and which opened the door to the creation of other types of domains. In the case of Wikipedia, the Amical Viquipèdia group of friends of the Catalan Wikipedia lobbied the Wikimedia Foundation to create the Thematic Organizations[2], which were local chapters of Wikimedia based on common interests and not borders. Up until that point, only national chapters had existed.

The Catalan version of Wikipedia is world renowned for its relationships with various cultural institutions, thanks to the GLAMwiki initiative[3], which has facilitated such connections. We have collaborated with world famous institutions like the Picasso Museum, the Joan Miró Foundation, the Dalí Theatre-Museum, the Catalan National Art Museum, and the network of libraries of the Catalan government. When we present such projects in conferences and workshops around the world, people always ask us why we write them in Catalan, instead of in Spanish or French. After we explain what Catalonia is, we also add that Catalans are at the very least bilingual and that it would be very easy to consult or write a wiki in Spanish, French, or Italian—languages with a much larger audience potential—but that that would probably be a death sentence for our language in the medium term.

They are also surprised that we are able to achieve this level of engagement among cultural institutions and volunteer editors. In Europe, most of the museums and libraries were created out of royal collections, but not in Catalonia, where it was the civil society that took the initiative and created its own social and cultural networks. That's why it's in the DNA of our cultural institutions to collaborate with everyday citizens. It connects perfectly with the wiki spirit. If we don't do it, nobody will. And if you want something to exist, create it yourself, and share it with others.

The beauty of it all is that we are an open community. We Catalan editors routinely collaborate with any initiative that begins on a global scale. Within the Wikipedian community, they know us as the *Catalan Army* because we are always the most active participants in the world and whenever we can, we help with translations or whatever is needed[4]. Even the BBC has noticed our efforts and reported on the Catalan Wikipedia. Once again, our only weapon for winning the world's confidence has been our work.

---

2 http://meta.wikimedia.org/wiki/Wikimedia_CAT

3 http://theglamwikiexperience.blogspot.com/

4 https://commons.wikimedia.org/wiki/Category:GLAM_in_Catalonia

The languages of the Catalans

M. Carme Junyent

Professor of General Linguistics at the University of Barcelona, founder of the Study Group for Threatened Languages. Director of various research projects on immigrants' languages, including an inventory of languages that are spoken in Catalonia. Commissioner of several expositions on linguistic diversity. Member of the Expert Committee on the Universal Declaration of Linguistic Rights.

"If I tell someone in Madrid that I speak Quechua, nobody pays attention. If I say it in Catalonia, everyone asks me questions about it." A Catalan of Bolivian extraction sums up in this way one of the characteristics often attributed to Catalan society: the value that is given to language. For many years, the debate about language was centered around the relationship between Spanish and Catalan, but in recent years, Catalonia has experienced a spectacular demolinguistic change that has touched both rural areas and urban ones. During the first decade of the 21st century, more than 1 million immigrants moved to Catalonia from all over the world. During this period, the population went from 6 million to 7.5 million, and the number of languages with speakers in Catalonia rose to almost 300.[1]

The reactions to this phenomenon can be divided into two big groups: those who have related the newly arrived Catalans with the dominant language, and have added them to the Spanish block, and those who in one way or another have associated them with Catalan, if at least as a source of new speakers. It's important to point out that this perception to a great degree has been encouraged by the newcomers themselves. On the one hand, we have those that, without any prior knowledge of their destination, thought they were coming to Spain, and thus to a Spanish-speaking place, and on the other, those that established a symmetry with the linguistic situation of the place they came from.

In this second case, the mirroring has often led to identification with the new place, since many of the newcomers are speakers of subordinate languages in their areas of origin, and in some cases, say that they have "discovered" their own language in Catalonia. That is, in the process of identifying with Catalan, they have also been able to recognize their own language, the need to recover it if it has been lost, or to revalue it, both of which result in a growth in self-esteem. It's obvious that adopting Catalan offers many benefits, not only economic, but particularly social and emotional. As Sándor Márai says, "The children of all small nationalities feel honored when a stranger makes the effort to speak their mother tongue."[2] And Catalonia is a small nationality that not only feels honored but in many cases empathizes with the linguistic history of other small nationalities. Naturally, this is not a universal trait, and once more, we can separate out two tendencies in the attitude

1 The Study Group for Threatened Languages of the University of Barcelona has inventoried a total of 278 languages spoken in Catalonia.

2 Márai, S. (1943) *La Gavina*, Ed. Empúries, Barcelona, 2011, p. 17.

toward other peoples' languages: one of indifference and one of empathy (hostility is frankly receding).

The difference in these attitudes toward the languages spoken by Catalans are revealed in different areas, and particularly in the context of education. It's obvious that the growth that Catalan society has experienced has also been evident in the schools, where the number of foreign-born students rose from 19,793 in the 1999–2000 school year to 155,845 in the 2009–2010 school year.[3] A good number of these students attended "welcome classes", a space created to facilitate their adaptation to the curriculum, to give personalized emotional support, and to give intensive instruction in the Catalan language. In these classes, more than 100 different first languages have been identified. The Service for Linguistic Immersion and Welcome has also organized language courses for these first languages, a pioneering and practically unheard of initiative in other parts of the State, that any student may participate in. Classes have been given in Amazigh, Arab, Bengali, Chinese, Dutch, Portuguese, Quechua, Romanian, Ukrainian, and Urdu.

Beyond attending to the newly arrived students, however, the awareness of the linguistic diversity itself has been gradually introduced into the curriculum, so that all of the students can incorporate the knowledge offered by their classmates. It is here that a great difference is revealed, depending on the teacher's specialty. In a research project currently being carried out[4] in which teachers are asked which languages are spoken in their school, it has been noticed that, generally, it's the Catalan-language teachers who are more aware of these other languages, and that there is little difference between the awareness of teachers of other languages (Spanish, English, and French) and those of other teachers of other subjects. In the area of adult education, it was precisely the Consortium for Linguistic Normalization (the organization in charge of teaching the Catalan language outside of the school system) who inventoried the languages of the students, something that had not been carried out by any other organizations that also offer language courses (such as the Red Cross, Cáritas [Charity], and so on) regardless of whether they were Spanish or Catalan.

Catalan society, therefore, is making an important effort to incorporate this diversity and not make it an obstacle to getting along. It's very clear that

---

3 Source: Service for Linguistic Immersion and Welcoming, Department of Education, Government of Catalonia.

4 The role of immigrant languages in school. Project financed by the Ministry of Science and Innovation. FFI2009–05995.

their own linguistic history is reflected in these efforts. The experience of living in a stigmatized language is brought home when a new immigrant speaks about their own language as a "dialect" or a "primitive language". There is special appreciation when someone learns a language that others may have decided is nonessential.

The challenge now is knowing how to treat this diversity in an independent Catalonia. Whatever the future brings, there is one thing that is clear: there will be languages from all over the world in the family history of a very high percentage of Catalans. How the future will turn out will also depend on how we treat these languages now, and it doesn't seem like most political leaders have this in mind. Both Mas and Junqueras, the two leaders with the most seats in Parliament, have announced their support of official status for Spanish in an independent Catalonia. In other words, both of them continue to foresee a bilingual Catalonia while ignoring the 12 percent of the population that has *neither Spanish nor Catalan* as its first language. If we take into account that some 46 percent of newly arrived immigrants, according to the Secretary for Immigration for the Government of Catalonia, are in favor of independence, it doesn't seem very astute to ignore their contribution to a country that shouldn't want to suppress diversity or to reproduce in a portion of its citizens the same situation that has made many of us feel rejected by Spain.

Non-nationalist independentism

Laura Borràs

Ph.D. in Romance Philology (1997) from the University of Barcelona. Awarded special Ph.D. Prize on Humanities and Social Sciences (1998). Borràs lectures in Literary Theory and Comparative Literature as well as a Teacher Education Masters Degree program at the University of Barcelona. Since 2000, she has coordinated the international research group HERMENEIA, which studies connections between literary studies and digital technologies. In January, 2013, she was appointed Director of the Institution of Catalan Literature of the Government of Catalonia.

A few years ago, independentists were viewed—both in public and private conversations—as crazy dreamers. The comments generated by the independence movement in Madrid (as a simplification for all Spanish unionists), but also in a mostly reticent Catalonia were generally full of scorn. To minimize their possible social impact and, at the same time with the perverse intention of neutralizing their ideological power, pro-independence activists were always referred to as just a mere handful of people. Perhaps. But that handful has now obeyed the divine commandments to "be fruitful and multiply". Those idealistic youths have grown up (and become respectable!), and even the ones who haven't gone into politics have at least decided to stand up politically. And although, in the words of the Catalan pop group Manel, "it's taken God and some extra help to get here", here we are. Many myths have been deconstructed along the way (economic dependency on exports belied by boycotts, comparisons of the Spanish and international markets, and so on) and there has even been time for some political debate—some successful, some not so much—that corroborates the fact that we are facing an option that is ever larger and all-embracing. What the polls confirm today and that Catalans can confirm by just looking around them is that independentism has become an undeniable reality.

There has been some important help along the way. Spain's reactions toward Catalonia in the last few years—vis à vis the Statute of Autonomy, rulings of the Spanish Constitutional Court, linguistic interference, sports contests, and so on—have been natural catalysts toward the growth of pro-independence sensibilities. The systematic scorn and plundering continues unabated in all areas: linguistic, political, cultural, artistic, sporting, and of course, economic. The sports example is crystal clear. The maxim that politics and sport must never be mixed is brandished, paradoxically, by those who are best at mixing them. Considering them to be unmixable is just the rhetoric and the easy fallacy that despite its overuse never seems to fall out of fashion. The Spanish press is a specialist at giving master lessons in the combination thereof. And it does so every week, while showcasing the Formula 1, or motorcycle racing, or the NBA in which "Spaniards" are prominent. The very concept of "national team" is a political concept, and sporting competitions, starting with the Olympic Games themselves, are as well.

The problem, as ever, is knowing where your nationalism ends and where the other guy's starts. To *politicize*, according to Merriam-Webster is "to give a political tone or character <an attempt to *politicize* the civil service>". So what must we then infer about requiring athletes to play for a team they don't feel to be their own, fining them if they refuse, expelling them for defending "other" national teams within the same state, or brandishing the Spanish passport as an argument for excluding the Catalan Hockey Federation from the International Federation of Roller Sports, among many other examples. In short, Catalonia is prohibited from having its own national teams. Is that not politicizing sport?

That is precisely how the Spanish government has devoted its energy, to the point of being the poster child for the tired bromide on the topic: What nationality is listed on your ID card? (Hearing this question is a clear indication that it is no longer useful to discuss the matter with the person who has asked and who wields such a hefty weapon.) Their argument is that Catalan athletes are Spanish because that's what their passport says. Clap, clap, clap. Very convincing. But they make this effort, and risk looking foolish, because they are aware that the public and private spheres are very important. And we know that the participants are political. Sport serves to create a national identity that is expressed with particular cultural values. Do chants of USA! USA! sound familiar? This has always been the case, without exception.

What is harder to stomach is when being "one of us" is a sign of normalcy and when being "one of them" is a demonstration of exclusive extremism. When they yell "Long Live Spain!" and when we yell "Long Live Barça and Long Live Catalonia!" we are all strengthening our national conscience. But consciences are an expensive commodity and the impression is that some are first rate, and others are seconds. Or as Tísner, whose 100th birthday we celebrated in 2012, noted bitterly, "We have a deplorable tendency of giving in. We are a people who has never had a national conscience." Joan Sales (another of those who was commemorated in 2012) said "one even ends up suspecting that everyone in the world outside of Catalonia is a patriot, that would explain why we continue to regress after 400 years". And further, "We Catalans have spent the last 300 years playing the fool. But that doesn't mean we have to stop being Catalan, we just have to stop playing the fool." It is a sad commentary from Sales who considered himself Catalan "just like an apricot feels like an apricot and not a peach". Well, let's see if we're ready to apply that to ourselves, and finally stop acting like peaches.

The worldwide economic crisis, and with it, the budget cuts, have helped increase the bad feelings. Today, the sovereigntist option is increasingly put on the table, which is not surprising if you take into account that the difference between what is paid and what is received continues to grow. The big question is "if we have a GDP that is comparable to various prosperous countries, why is our actual level of well-being below that of many Spanish regions?" The wealth that Catalonia generates is not reflected in its subsequent well-being. At any rate, not for those Catalans famously defined by long-time former president Jordi Pujol as *those that live and work in Catalonia*. This fact promotes pragmatic, not nationalistic, independentism.

A Spanish emigrant, and there are many, will not stop feeling Spanish because they live abroad, but instead will look out for their interests where they live, work, and receive services in exchange for their taxes. Why should it be any different? Maybe it's not necessary to be sentimental, but rather radically pragmatic, which in times of crisis, is doubly necessary. In a global world like the one in which we live, independence need not be a question that only concerns identity. Unless I'm mistaken, they have yet to discover detectors that can reveal the secrets of the heart, as Catalan singer Lluís Llach sang in "País petit" (small country), while the secrets of the pocketbook are already old news to the people, and the experts say it's unsustainable.

The Spanish colonies overseas needed 300 years to culminate their struggle for freedom and each celebrates its national day on the day they became independent. We're close to our own 300th anniversary of Catalonia's defeat in 1714, the moment of the symbolic but effective, definitive, and total collapse of Catalonia at Castile's (not Spain's) feet. This led Castile to convert itself, by force, into what we now call Spain, with its characteristic features: the prohibition of Catalan and the imposition of Spanish as the only language. It's been 300 years since our institutions (the Council of One Hundred, the *Generalitat*, the *Diputació*), our flag, and our language were the leaders, and not regional, or secondary. How much longer do we have to live this constant schizophrenia? How much longer do we have to pretend that we don't realize that fitting in with Spain is a joke? How much longer do we have to bear the paradox of having to ask for money from the folks who take our money away? Will we realize that independence is a state of political, cultural, and economic emancipation and that sovereignty is equally necessary for us as it is for all who have been able to shake off the yoke of a plundering state? Civil society is always one step ahead of the politicians in terms of independence, that much is clear. Today we need politicians who wish to make history for making a significant contribution to their country: making the independence of Catalonia possible.

Catalan language literature: What's going on?

Matthew Tree

Based in Barcelona since 1984. Tree has published 10 books written in Catalan, including two novels, a collection of short stories, an autobiography, a rant against work, and a personal essay on racism. In English, he has published the collection of articles and essays Barcelona, Catalonia. A View From the Inside *(2011). His agent in Barcelona is about to publish a promotional edition of his new novel in English,* Snug.

The first time I went—or rather, was taken—to a Catalan bookshop, back in 1978, I wasn't even sure that there was such a thing as Catalan literature. From then on, from that first sight of the gleaming covers covering the tables at the La Tralla bookshop in Vic (central Catalonia), I've been reading in Catalan, moving from one surprise to the next.

The first book in Catalan I read wasn't written in Catalonia or by a Catalan. *Diccionari per a ociosos* (1964; an English translation appeared in 2006: *Dictionary for the Idle*, Five Leaves Publications, Nottingham) was by Joan Fuster, an essayist from the Valencian area. The next book I read was a collection of short stories by Carme Riera, a native Mallorcan. Over the years, perhaps a good third of the Catalan originals I've read have been written outside the limits of the Principality itself but within the confines of the Catalan-speaking areas as a whole, which are both transregional and transnational: French Catalonia, Andorra, Valencia, southern Aragon, and the Balearic Islands.

Not only that, but I came to realize that many of the bona fide Catalan writers I was starting to discover—that is to say, authors born within the Principality—wrote some of their best work thousands of miles away. Exiled after Franco's victory in 1939—after which it was as dangerous, within Spain, to be a Catalan language writer as it was to be an anarcho-syndicalist—Pere Calders wrote his extraordinary short stories and novels (imbued with what would later be called magical realism) in Mexico. Mercè Rodoreda wrote her internationally acclaimed classic *In Diamond Square* (the third English translation of which will appear later this year) in Geneva; the surreal humorist Francesc Trabal's last novel was completed in Santiago de Chile, and so on, and so forth.

In other words, Catalan literature was and is by definition multinational, a global project, so to speak, and not in any way a regional literature in the sense that most people give to that term: parochial, rural-orientated, of merely local interest. On the contrary, I found myself getting a sneaky kind of pleasure from the realization that I was reading world-class writing in a language that most people didn't know and that was still little translated (a situation which, as we shall see, has changed considerably).

Although what I couldn't imagine, during those first years of reading in Catalan, was that, with time, Catalan writers would appear on the scene who hadn't even been born anywhere in the Catalan-speaking areas and for whom Catalan was a second or third, language. And yet, since the early 1990s, we have seen the appearance of the Slovenian essayist Simona Skrabec; the

Czech novelist and translator Monika Zgustova; the Iraqi autobiographer Pius Alibek; the Palestinian novelist, historian, and cookery expert Salah Jamal; the American literary critic Sam Abrams; the Beninese expert on children's stories and West African cuisine Agnès Agboton; the excellent Morocco-born novelist Najat El Hachmi; and the Argentinian journalist and novelist Patrícia Gabancho—all of them writing and publishing directly in Catalan.

As a result of all this border-crossing and variety, we can find just about every type of fiction imaginable within the Catalan literary panorama of the last hundred years or so: crime fiction, science fiction, historical fiction, made-to-measure bestsellers, popular literary fiction, cult literary fiction, erotic fiction, autobiographical fiction, and so on in a host of settings on the five continents. Romanticism, Modernism, Realism, Existentialism, Surrealism, Minimalism, Post-modernism, Post-post-modernism, and just about any other kind of Western literary tendency that might come to mind, all will be found to have their representatives within modern Catalan literature.

What is more, translation into Catalan (as well as Spanish, which all Catalans can also read perfectly well) has ensured that a wide range of international authors are directly available to Catalan language writers. Many such authors, indeed, are often translated into Catalan years before they reach an English language audience (Jonathan Littell and Yannick Haennel, for example) or never do reach an English language audience at all (for example, there are more titles by the Czech Bohumil Hrabal or the Portuguese António Lobo Antunes, available in Catalan than there are in English). Indeed, Catalan has often put me in better touch with recent international writing than has English.

Round about the time—toward the end of the eighties—when it had become quite clear to me that Catalan literature was swimming with the best of them in the European mainstream and was not some kind of self-referential sop for a handful of bookish yokels, I got an unsolicited house call from a salesman for a cultural organization that sold Catalan books and music. He opened his patter with the question: "Do you like Catalan culture?" which made about as much sense to me as asking if I liked Catalan vegetables. Catalan culture—especially its language-based products—is simply too vast and heterogeneous to be lumped together into a single unit.

How to describe it, then? How to provide some kind of inclusive overview? Well, one option is to take the academic road and simply describe its chronological progress (which is what the English professor Arthur Terry did in his excellent work, *Companion to Catalan Literature* [2003]).

According to Terry and most other historians, then, Catalan literature made its first appearance around about 1260 (though written religious and administrative documents in the language date from the 10th century on). It was this period that ushered in the work of the poet, philosopher, and fabulist Ramon Llull; that of Ausiàs March (almost certainly the first major poet to write individual love poems in any European vernacular) and—albeit somewhat later, in the 15th century—the first great European proto-novel, Joanot Martorell's *Tirant lo Blanc*. Around these three major figures buzz a host of only slightly lesser writers of prose, poetry, and historical narrative: Ramon Muntaner, Roís de Corella, Jaume Roig, Bernat Metge, Arnau de Vilanova, Anselm Turmeda, Francesc Eiximenis, and Jordi de Sant Jordi. The list goes on and on, given that medieval Catalan literature was, quite simply, one of the finest—and most prolific—in Europe.

But with the 16th century, according to our standard academic plotline, came a steep swoop into decline for Catalan literature, coinciding with the political decline of the courts of Valencia and Barcelona. Among what would now be called intellectuals, Castilian (Spanish)—the language of a literary golden age centered on the now uniquely powerful Castilian nobility—began to provide literary models that Catalan language writers followed, when they didn't directly adopt Castilian as their literary language. What was more, after 1714—when Catalonia was incorporated by force of arms into the fledgling Spanish State—the Catalan universities were shut down, and the language was banned (over the following decades) in schools, courts, churches, and books, leading to a further process of *castilianization* and a corresponding further decline in Catalan literary output.

Then, in the mid 19th century, came the period known as the *Renaixença* ("Renaissance"), a time of romanticized national revival when many Catalan authors rediscovered their medieval literary heritage. Poetry and prose fiction (as well as books based on historical and folkloric research into Catalonia's past and present, respectively) appeared with increasing frequency. Some of the work produced—the novels of Narcís Oller, the poetry of Jacint Verdaguer, the plays of Àngel Guimerà—were of a quality not seen since the late medieval period and are still widely read (and translated) today.

The unevenness of the work produced during the *Renaixença* eventually led to the first genuinely consistent period of Catalan literature in the modern age, when the *Modernista* movement—which gave a quasi-mystic, emotional hue to much Catalan writing—got going towards the end of the 19th century. From here on until 1939, Catalan literature branched out into various tendencies and schools but never ceased to be recognizable as a single flourishing, modern European literature with dozens of writers of talent or even genius: the painter, dramatist and novelist Santiago Rusiñol; the novelist Raimon Casellas; the outstanding poet and essayist Joan Maragall; the Mallorcan poet Joan Alcover; the elitist columnist and novelist Eugeni d'Ors; the great surrealist poet JV Foix; the author Catalina Albert (better known by her pen name of Víctor Català); the poet Josep Carner; the prose master Josep Pla; and the novelist and poet Josep Maria de Segarra.

All of this ended with an outsize jolt when Franco and his rebel subordinates entered Catalonia in 1939. Franco and the regime he was about to spawn perceived Catalonia to be the single greatest threat to Spanish unity, precisely because of the vitality of Catalan, a language he immediately banned everywhere outside the home (though even at home, one could be arrested for having books in Catalan). Catalan literature had to be either published abroad or in clandestine or semi-clandestine form within Catalonia itself. The distribution networks, the magazines, the reviews, and the public debates that had kept the literature so very much alive disappeared completely. In 1961, the State loosened its restrictions somewhat and made it possible to publish more titles and translations in Catalan, but by now two generations were literate in Spanish only and found reading Catalan hard-going. Remarkably, a large handful of Catalan writers stubbornly refused to change to Spanish, so that when Catalan became a legally teachable language once more, after Franco's death in 1976, people snapped up the poetry and prose not only of the pre-war writers but also of those who had started writing in the second half of the 20th century: Terenci Moix, Salvador Espriu, Montserrat Roig, Pere Calders, Manuel de Pedrolo, and many others.

A younger generation of writers took Catalan writing into the new millennium, notably the short story writers and columnists Quim Monzó and Sergi Pàmies. In short, the current literary panorama in Catalan is now much the same as it is in any other European language: a blend of successful literary fiction, with titles such as Jordi Puntí's *Lost Luggage* or Najat El Hachmi's *The Body Hunter* (both to be available soon in English), bestsellers such as Martí Gironell's *L'últim abat (The Last Abbot),* and a host of nonfiction titles ranging from Patrícia Gabancho's memoirs of her family in Buenos Aires to titles dealing with the current push for political independence, which have become a kind of genre in their own right.

At the same time, new writers are appearing every other month, often published by a new slew of small presses that have started to compete with the less experimental but larger and better established publishing houses.

Having said which, I personally, for what that's worth, have never held much faith in the idea of literary progression—one movement or tendency following another. Writers of any age, in the end, no matter how they may deliberately copy existing or pre-existing models, are, when all is said and done, on their own: individuals firing from permanently vulnerable positions. Writing is, therefore, nothing if not a process confined to the individual and the individual, by definition, has no choice in the last resort but to do what he or she thinks best (and then hope for the best). Catalan writers are no exception. No matter what their political ideologies might be—and in an area as highly politicized as the Catalan-speaking lands, it is almost inevitable that they feel the need to adopt some kind of political stance—their best fiction is like good fiction anywhere: it takes no sides, it explores the gray areas of human life, it abhors the judgmental. Those writers who feel a wish to do so express their political opinions in works of nonfiction or in blogs and newspaper columns and chat shows. When they return to their novels and short stories, they are once again free to re-enter the ambiguous realm of the uncertain in which most of us seem to live.

If I seem to be harping on this, I do so to dispel a commonly held brickbat about authors who choose to write in Catalan: that they do so for political ("nationalist") reasons, and that this therefore taints their literary production. Quim Monzó (whose mother, by the way, was Andalusian) put this straight in the 1980s, in an interview with the *Avui* newspaper: "I'm not nationalist, or any nonsense like that; the thing is, I'm not Spanish."

Aha.

Catalonia or Catalan Countries?

Vicent Sanchis

Degree in Information Sciences from the Autonomous University of Barcelona. Professor in Journalism in the Blanquerna School of the Ramon Llull University. Editor of several publications, including the Avui *newspaper for 12 years, and television programs. Currently editor/ publisher of the magazine* El Temps *and collaborator and columnist in both print and digital newspapers. Winner of the Joan Fuster Prize for Non-fiction with the book* Franco contra Flash Gordon [Franco versus Flash Gordon] *and the Carles Rahola Prize with* Valencians, encara [Still Valencian].

What is the *Catalan Nation* and what does that expression even mean? Most of the visitors who come to Catalonia each year are tourists and they don't have the slightest idea. At the best, maybe they've heard of Gaudí or Barça. And that Gaudí and Barça are the highest expressions of art and sports, respectively, of a land, Catalonia, that is a region, a part of Spain. A Spain that has expressed itself exclusively in Spanish and whose most recognized and celebrated characteristics are bullfighting and flamenco dancing. Even today. There are so many people who never have the chance to notice a different reality. A more genuine "difference". There are many more who go back home without having heard a word of the Catalan language. And those who return home with a few broad superficial strokes that simply confirm the few stereotypes they brought with them. And they do it with an Andalusian guitar, a bullfighter's hat, or an Andalusian doll that they bought on the Rambles in Barcelona as the most representative expression of what is "Made in Spain". Or even worse: sometimes the souvenir with which they remember their journey is a sombrero from Mexico!

But it is also increasingly true that some of these visitors, before they step foot in Catalonia have received news about a different reality. One that affirms that Catalonia is not a region, but an old European nation that gets on the best it can—and over the centuries has made the best of—living in a state called Spain. A state that hides within various diverse national realities, especially from the outside world. That tries to dilute them. This knowledge, that destroys old preconceptions and stereotypes, has grown steadily since 1.5 million Catalans came out to demonstrate on September 11, 2012, demanding the independence of Catalonia. Regions don't demand independence. Only nations do. Given this logic, some of the visitors and the curious now close in on the Catalan reality from a new perspective, with different information facilitated to them by the media of their own countries. It is in this way that Catalans are beginning to be known internationally as a "special case". Like the Irish, the Scotch, or the Quebeckers.

But now that we've gotten to this point, which just a short time ago seemed so difficult to reach, it's time to go one step farther. The definition of the Catalan Nation is neither mathematic nor singular. For most Catalans who live in the four Spanish administrative provinces that have their own autonomous regime—called *Catalonia*—the Catalan Nation goes no farther than that territory: Tarragona, Lleida, Girona and Barcelona. A country that on geographical maps of the Iberian Peninsula is bordered by the Pyrenees mountains and the Ebre and Sénia Rivers. But the political Catalanism—from the time of Enric Prat de la Riba (1870–1917) one of its most influential theorizers—often proposed a different reality. More complicated and more difficult still.

A reality that comprises all of the territories where Catalan is spoken and that from the 12th until the 18th century formed a political unit called the *Crown of Aragon*. A unit formed by various territories—the Principality of Catalonia, Aragon, the Kingdom of Valencia and the Kingdom of Mallorca—forged from the Christian conquest of the Muslim territories from the Pyrenees onward in a long process that began in the 9th century and didn't end until the 13th. Each with their own laws and privileges that were abolished after their defeat in the so-called War of the Spanish Succession (1701–1715).

Presently, those territories make up distinct "autonomous communities" within the current territorial structure of the Spanish State, in force since the approval of the Constitution of 1978. There is, therefore an "autonomous community" of Catalonia, one of Valencia, one of the Balearic Islands, and one of Aragon. There are also a few counties around the city of Perpignan that Spain ceded to France as a consequence of one of the wars the two countries had in the 17th century and which now belong to French *départements*. All of these territories, colonized by Catalans, shared—and continue to share today—the Catalan language and culture.

And it is this common language and this common culture which distinguish and define our different nation. A concept that, in present-day terms, incorporates not only "Catalonia" but also the Valencian Country, the Balearic Islands, the part of Catalonia administered by France, and a long strip of Aragonese territory that also has Catalan as its language. The concept, therefore, of a Catalan nation is even wider. There are a lot of people who reduce it to a strictly cultural environment. The "Catalan nation" is for them, a cultural phenomenon—like *Francophonie* is for the French.

There are also a lot of people who demand such a definition politically. There are many Valencians, Mallorcans, Menorcans, or Aragonese who feel nationally "Catalan". The most brilliant defender in favor of this political option is the Valencian writer Joan Fuster (1922–1992). Joan Fuster was in favor of the old political union between Catalans, Mallorcans, and Valencians as the only viable alternative to the disappearance of the nation. As a single valid answer to the pretensions of being diluted as "Spanish"—of Spanish language and culture. A pretension that the crown and the State has spent centuries trying to achieve. Without success so far.

Time to say "yes"

Eva Piquer

Writer, cultural journalist, mother of four, Member of the Catalan Parliament. Formerly subdirector of culture at the daily Avui, *Professor of Journalism at the Autonomous University of Barcelona and correspondent in New York. Piquer has collaborated in various media, and is member of the Advisory Council for the magazine* Catalan International View. *Piquer won the Josep Pla Prize for her novel* Una victòria diferent [A Different Victory] *(2002) and the Atlàntida Prize for best columnist in Catalan. She has published several other books, the most recent of which is* Petita història de Barcelona [A Short History of Barcelona] *(2012).*

When I was little they tricked me. They brought me to a school where they educated us as if we lived in a normal country. Smack in the middle of the Franco era, which is saying something. In that extraordinary school—where we had a portrait of the dictator hidden in the attic, and they ran to hang it when an inspector came to call—they made us believe that the equality of men and women really existed. And that Catalonia was a country just like any other and that Catalan was a completely normalized language.

So when I was little, I never felt any need to be Catalanist, or feminist, or progressive. Those battles had already been won, and life was too short to spend insisting on what we already had.

But one sad day, I left the bubble in which I had grown up and I discovered that they had lied to me. That nothing was done yet. That we still had to talk about equality in the future tense, that it wasn't true that the women of my generation had it all. That progressivism was under siege on all sides. And no, we didn't live in a normal country.

I should've been mad for all those years I grew up deceived. But I wasn't. On the one hand, I was so grateful to my parents for having sent me to the Arrel school, making all manner of sacrifices—my parents were from a humble background and the monthly tuition wasn't exactly cheap. (I spent my youth demanding that we wanted to be a public school, and in the end, we did it!) And on the other hand, I didn't get mad because there was no time to waste. What was necessary was to roll up my sleeves and keep fighting. What could I do? I became a feminist. And a progressive. And a Catalanist. That is, an independentist. I wanted to live in a free country.

When I was a teenager, I joined the *Crida a la Solidaritat en Defensa de la Llengua* (Cry for Solidarity in Defense of the Language), a grass-roots movement that tried to change the world with happiness. We were the ones who painted ships pink, who filled the airport with paper airplanes to demand its catalanization, or who traveled in the "Nations Train" to Strasburg to demand that Catalan be an official language in Europe. It was fun in the Crida, and I even appreciated the earlier generations who had left us some road to travel. I even said once that I had been born too late, that I would've liked being born in the fifties so I could have rebelled against Francoism, so I could have run from the police.

I remember an argument I used to have with a good friend, 25 or so years ago. I told him that I would've liked to experience the adrenaline rush at the end of the dictatorship and he said that what I was saying made no sense at all. He was right, because there are always new causes to fight for.

Positively and happily, peacefully, but to fight for. Right now, I want to leave the best world possible for my four children. And I have no doubt that, if they want, they'll find ways to make it even better.

Later, I became a journalist. Theoretically, we journalists are not supposed to come out politically. You're supposed to appear neutral, and if you say how you really feel, you're sunk. They hang a tag on you, and you lose credibility. It's true that we all play politics, in all areas. Even those who say they're completely apolitical, well you'll excuse me if I don't get how they do it. Because if you're an atheist and you don't believe in the other world, well that's your problem and maybe God or whoever will punish you once you're on the other side. But to not be interested in how we organize ourselves in this life, which is the only one we're sure we have, that just seems strange to me. We are all political, but to be open about it often leads to criticism. It's not accepted. One of our national sports is to speak badly about politicians. As if they were all corrupt and all worked against the people. And that just cannot be, if for no other reason than that it is statistically impossible.

There comes a time, though, when you get the feeling that you have to roll up your sleeves even further. That you have to speak out. Because it is an exceptional moment, and exceptional situations require exceptional attitudes. And that moment is now. I still pinch myself every morning to make sure that I'm not dreaming and that it's really true that we're finally getting closer to the longed for independence, which means normalcy, which means being responsible for ourselves, which means being whatever we want to be. We are moving toward being a normal country. We just want to be what we are, nothing more. A friend told me the other day that she is scared that we're building a country that is not a paradise. Look, at least it will be ours, and if there is misery, it'll be *our* misery.

The world is divided into three types of people. People who do things, people who don't do things and also don't let other people do things, and the immense majority of us who look at each other, and depending on the vibes that we get or give from one group or another, we get down to work, or we look the other way, to keep them from making us load boxes, sell raffle tickets, or clear the table. There are also three kinds of fathers and mothers: those who are the presidents of the PTA, those who never even go to the meetings and those who go out of inertia but end up getting put on the School Traffic Committee because they understand that they have to get the streetlight installed at that dangerous intersection and that, if they don't get involved, they won't have any right to complain later.

It's time to fight for that green light that's going to bring us freedom. We Catalans realize that we are at a historic crossroads. We can either accept the path of humiliation and collective suicide—which is what awaits us if we stick with Spain—or we move toward national liberation. And we have come to the conclusion that there is no conflicted choice to make: sick of having to ask for permission and apologize for our existence, and heirs of a dignity that thankfully we haven't completely lost, we have no other option than to grab the torch from the generations that went before us and move forward with a firm step toward the only possible goal. We have no other choice than to shuck off the comfortable positions, and to commit ourselves from head to toe, because we're betting the future of our children and our children's children. Our life is in the balance and we have to act accordingly.

We are living in decisive moments. And in moments like this one, you and I and the upstairs neighbor all have to roll up our sleeves. Because clearing the table is a job for one, but building a country is a project that requires an incredible joint effort. The responsibility is so enormous that we have to back up our professional politicians: we in the community can't just wash our hands of the whole affair. We're only going to make it through if we all push together in the same direction. And the world only changes from the inside. Independence (or a sovereign state, or however you want to call it) is not going to get here if we sit on the sofa waiting for it to come. Independence, which means freedom, has to be earned.

Now is the time to go for it. And to get it, of course, but it would be crazy to not try for it when we finally have the best opportunity of the last 300 years. Or in all of history. Now is the time, I think, to fight for that green light that we have wanted for so long. That's why I'm so excited that a historic and future-minded political party like Esquerra Republicana [Republican Left], a sovereigntist and leftist party, asked me to help them push from the inside, as an independent. They offered to include me on ERC's lists for the Catalan Parliamentary elections and I dared to say yes, because now is the time to say yes. On the referendum too, of course. Now is the time to build ourselves positively and to emancipate ourselves once and for all, and to have our own voice in this world that belongs to everyone. We cannot lose any more time depending on Spain.

I don't want independence because it's a lesser evil, because they treat us badly, or because we don't have any other choice. I want independence with happiness. Because we're grownups now and we want to be responsible for ourselves. Like I heard Salvador Cardús, the sociologist, say once, "I would want independence even if it meant we lost money." And as Oriol Junqueras says, "I would be for independence even if Spain were the most prosperous country on earth." Which it's not, just for the record.

But now, in addition, independence is a necessity. An emergency. It's stopped being a utopia and started being the only possible solution that will allow us to remake and maintain our state of well being. To be able to have a country with doctors, schools, jobs, and opportunities. Today in Catalonia there are almost 1 million people out of work, and that includes one out of every two young people.

Today we pay for a state that ends up costing us dearly, and it plays against us to boot: it doesn't want us to decide for ourselves, it attacks our language, it doesn't invest in Catalonia, and it skims off 16 billion euros every year. Meanwhile, the Spanish State squanders millions and millions of euros on trains that don't bring anyone anywhere, on airports with no airplanes. It's normal and legitimate that we want to administer what is ours. It's normal that we want to do what, in the last century, 29 of the 50 states in Europe have done: declare our independence. Not a single one of those states has any regrets: they are all happy to have a state to defend themselves with.

Without a fiscal deficit and with full sovereignty, we would all live better. The independentists—who will have stopped being independentists, hallelujah!—and those who aren't independentists. We would be, we *will* be the first new state in Europe that is born from a culmination of a completely democratic process, initiated by the democratic will of the people, a state that the people have earned. People who want to control their resources and their destiny. And it's to our advantage to carry out the process quickly and correctly, with democracy on our flag, because every month that goes by brings more unemployment, more debt, and more families that are barely hanging on in the misery.

We want a just society in a free country. We want a society, for example, that taxes the banks and the grand fortunes, that fights against fiscal fraud, and that doesn't systematically strangle the middle and working classes.

I have dedicated my whole life to cultural journalism and to books. In this new country that we have the opportunity of building, we'll have to be clear that culture is an essential value. And therefore, that it's not superfluous. We are the books that we have read, the paintings that we've contemplated, the songs that we've song. We can't do without culture because it's what civilizes us and which ends up giving meaning to what we do. Feeding ourselves intellectually is as essential as feeding the body. Whoever raises the VAT tax doesn't do it innocently, they do it because it's in their interest: a society that doesn't read is a more docile society, a more exploitable community.

We have to avoid reserving culture for only those who can pay for it. Maybe it has to have a price—because we live in a society that doesn't value what is free—and because if we don't pay for it, someone who wants us to consume precisely what is in their interests will pay. But it has to be a reasonable price. We have to defend the democratic access to culture. It has to be available for everyone, everywhere, because culture guarantees social cohesion and is the fourth leg of the welfare state.

In times of budget cuts, culture will have to be cut like everything else, but not more. Culture is both social policy and state structure. And investing in culture is proportionally so small (it's not even 1 percent of the entire budget of the Catalan government) that no matter how much you cut, it doesn't help that much, but you destroy the whole sector anyway. The annual culture budget is equivalent to what the Catalan government spends just on anxiety and anti-depressant medicine. We could do an experiment to see if investment in culture lowers the consumption of anti-depressants, because then people would be happier.

In an independent Catalonia, culture would be automatically reinforced, if for no other reason than because we would have more resources. And if our citizens had more consumer power, they would also consume more culture. And we wouldn't have a state that was against us, but rather one in favor, what a relief! One of my favorite poets, Joan Margarit, defends culture before liberty. Because without culture there is no liberty, even if you go vote every week, while if there is no liberty we can still have culture. Therefore, if we shout "Long live Catalonia!" (which we should also do) we should also shout "Long live a cultured Catalonia!" And as if that weren't enough, "Long live a fair Catalonia!"

One of the writers that I admire the most, Jaume Cabré, told me in 2010 when I interviewed him, "With our own state, we Catalans would be happier and we would live more calmly." That's why I want independence: I would be happier and I would live more calmly, since I wouldn't have to spend all my time and energy demanding the obvious, demanding permission, and apologizing for living.

Because I aspire to live in that fake world from when I was little, where I didn't have to be Catalanist or feminist or progressive, because those were all battles we had already won. And we had trouble at recess, of course, but at least nobody fought about whether the ball belonged to us. And nobody told us that the girls couldn't play football. We were what we wanted to be. Like we Catalans really soon, we're going to be what we want to be. And we can start living life, without having to waste another second demanding anything.

Another writer that I admire a lot, the poet and translator Montserrat Abelló, told me a little while before the November 25 elections that she was sure that she would see independence. She explains that when we are independent, Spanish will again be a beloved language. After the Spanish Civil War, Montserrat lived in exile in Chile for 20 years, and in the sixties she returned to Barcelona. And in Barcelona she found that Catalan was such a persecuted language that, as a reaction, she started hating Spanish. From that point forward, she hasn't read or worked anymore in Spanish, just in Catalan and English. And she's ready for independence so she can go back to loving a language that she had loved as much as she did Spanish. I think she'll be in time, and she's already 94. I love her optimism.

The hopeful will not save us from anything, but today we almost have the obligation of being optimistic. They say that the human brain starts out seeing the glass as half full. In order to survive, the majority have a slanted point of view of our own destiny. We are more optimists than realists. We undervalue the possibilities of breaking up with our partner, of losing our jobs, or of contracting some disease. Even if pessimism grows, private optimism will continue to grow. Deep down inside, everybody believes that he or she alone will end up being successful. That real misfortune will only happen to others.

The nice thing about having positive expectations is that just having them makes us happier. The optimists get divorced as much as the pessimists but they're more likely to get married again. They don't listen to lessons: hope trumps experience. And they value what they have, without worrying how long it will last. Having high expectations gets us closer to failure—we might crash—but it's the only thing that makes success possible.

The moment has arrived for us Catalans to be optimistic on a collective scale. From here on out we have the duty to see the glass more full than empty, to think that yes, we will achieve national liberation. We have to bury that old defeatist spirit, that "oh dear, oh dear" that is so us. It's an attitude that doesn't get us anywhere and that makes us lose before we have to. On September 11, 2012, so many people who came out to march were already preparing themselves for disappointment, they were sure that demonstrating wouldn't help anything. But boy, it really helped.

"This may turn out well," said Artur Mas last November 30, five days after the elections. We take the president's words and we turn the possibility into certainty: This will turn out well. Say it out loud, without reservations. This will turn out well. This will turn out well. This will turn out well. Who knows how and why we made it to this point in particular, but it turns out that we're at the door of that future that we have always wanted. We better start practicing, because celebration time might just be around the corner.

The so-called unionists want to scare us by saying we'll have to leave Europe and the euro and the metric system and the milky way, that we'll lose our pensions, that all the businesses will leave, and they'll boycott what's left, and who knows what else. We will need courage and patience and staying power. Although if they keep going at this rate, they're going to run out of scare tactics pretty quickly: we will get immunized and they won't be able to scare us ever again. But while they look for the new plague that will strike us down for becoming independent, we have to resist and counteract the fear with reason, with calm, and with democracy, lots of democracy. Nobody said it would be easy. But the easy challenges are not very exciting.

The objective in the balance is worth going for and we have the best opportunity in our history to get it. I want independence for my children, but I would also like my parents to see it. My parents, who were born after the war, children of the losers, a generation politically anesthetized by Francoism, who didn't develop a political conscience until the beginning of the seventies. And who then, at the beginning of the seventies wanted to give me the education that they couldn't have had, and sacrificed their budget in order to send me to that amazing school that made me believe, 40 years ago, that we lived in a normal country.

My first great political disappointment was the *Nacionalistes d'Esquerra* [Nationalists of the Left]. They were a pro-independence movement founded in 1979 who demanded the right of self-determination and sovereignty for Catalonia, in the framework of the Catalan Countries. My parents came home totally excited after a meeting: they had found their party. They brought me a poster from the campaign—with a verse about the party and about one of its leaders, Jordi Carbonell—that I hung above the headboard of my bed for a long time. When they held elections in 1980, I was eleven years old and I still didn't know I was a minority. I still hadn't made it out of my progressive, Catalanist, activist school's bubble. But reality is stubborn: 32 years ago, only 1.6 percent of Catalans bet on *Nacionalistes d'Esquerra*.

Now those of us who have been in favor of independence all our lives (convinced from the start that the only road toward a fair society passes through independence) feel a little strange: we haven't moved but the rest of the world has gotten closer. We've become the mainstream, who would've thought? And there are some who resent the newcomers. But what we need is for everyone to jump on the bandwagon, the more the merrier. The fact that the pro-independence starred flag is now carried around by everyone is great news. Because we will only win independence if independence is the choice of the majority. If we hold a referendum and yes wins. I have never voted for the winning party in an election but it sure would be nice to vote in a referendum and win. And for Jordi Carbonell, who'll be 90 in 2014, to be there, and Montserrat Abelló too, who's on her way to 100.

We will be what we want to be. On my Twitter profile it says "I have given birth to books, articles, and children". A friend told me not too long ago, "Pretty soon you're going to have to add that you helped give birth to a state." Wow. That would be a high point in my life. It will be a high point in all of our lives.

Long live Catalonia! Long live a cultured Catalonia! Long live a fair Catalonia!

A Scottish referendum for Catalonia

Xavier Solano

Diplomatic adviser in London and political aide to Scottish MPs at the UK Parliament. Has worked for Nicola Sturgeon when she became leader of the Scottish National Party at the Scottish Parliament and deputy to Alex Salmond, for the former Scottish Labour leader Wendy Alexander, and for the Scottish Government. He is the former Head of the Permanent Delegation of the Government of Catalonia to the UK, Ireland, and Iceland and the author of El mirall escocès [The Scottish Mirror] *(2007), a book on Scottish politics from a Catalan perspective. He has also published articles in several newspapers and magazines in Catalonia and has written chapters in several books.*

As matters currently stand, the referendums for the independence of Catalonia and Scotland are both likely to take place at some point in 2014. This is, without a shadow of a doubt, a historic moment, not just for Scotland, Catalonia, the UK, and Spain but also for the European Union. A positive outcome would lead to a process that in the end would result in the first truly internal enlargement in the history of the European Union—not counting the reunification of Germany back in 1990.

As the Scottish First Minister Alex Salmond wrote in the preface of my book *The Scottish Mirror* (RBA, 2007), "Scotland and Catalonia are old nations of Europe. We have written part of the history of Europe as free and independent countries."

Scotland and Catalonia have many things in common. Both are small nations that currently form part of European Union member states. Both lost their sovereignty at the beginning of the 18th century, Scotland in 1707 and Catalonia in 1714. Three hundred years later, a significant portion of both the Catalan and Scottish people believe that it no longer makes sense to remain within their respective states. The current situation no longer offers them sufficient benefits. Indeed, many believe that Scotland and Catalonia miss out on opportunities every day because they are not independent, and they do not have complete freedom to make decisions about their own affairs.

It turns out that there are more and more people who believe that it is time to become a grown-up nation, a people responsible for its own actions with all the associated consequences, just like the other approximately 200 countries in the world. There are many who believe that the Catalonia and Scotland of the future should have only two capitals, Brussels and their own, and that those decisions that are not made in Brussels should be taken in Barcelona or Edinburgh because, at the end of the day, independence is nothing more than having the freedom to make your own decisions and manage your own resources.

However, there are also important differences between Scotland and Catalonia. For instance, Scotland is considered a "nation" by the Government of the United Kingdom and the Scots are deemed to have the right to decide the future of Scotland. Its parliament is respected and trusted by the British Parliament of Westminster, which never legislates on matters that have been devolved to the Scottish Parliament. The budgets of the Scottish Parliament and Government are calculated through a transparent formula, the public revenue and expenditure reports are published regularly and the Scottish Parliament has full powers over the main policy areas such as education, health, or justice, to name just a few. Scotland also has official national teams competing internationally.

Catalonia has none of these. The Spanish government and parliament, unlike the British authorities with Scotland, have repeatedly refused to give such treatment and recognition to Catalonia.

There is another important difference between these two old nations. Scotland is a well known country. Most people have heard of Scotland or something connected to this country at some point in time. They might not know who Jack Vetriano is but surely most people have heard of Sean Connery, kilts, and exquisite Scotch whiskey.

It is different with Catalonia. Despite the fact that a fair number of our people, places, and organizations are quite well-known, few have ever heard of our thousand-year-old Catalan nation.

Some famous examples are the city of Barcelona and its unbeatable football (soccer) team, FC Barcelona, the renowned chef Ferran Adrià, the painters Salvador Dalí and Joan Miró, the cellist Pau Casals, the bubbly wine that we call *cava*, or even the beautiful Costa Brava. It is pretty hard to have never heard of anything Catalan or connected with Catalonia, but not so hard to miss that they are indeed Catalan.

Another thing that perhaps few people know is that Catalonia is a very old nation. For example, our current President, Mr. Artur Mas, is the 129th president of the *Generalitat* of Catalonia. To put this into context, allow me to compare this with the United States, whose current president, Barack Obama, is the 44th leader of that great nation. There are not many countries in the world that can claim that their first president was named in 1359. Obviously, the times have changed but the Catalans' sense of self-determination and sovereignty remain strong.

This desire for self-government is something we share with all of the nation-states in the world and also with those nations that, like Scotland, are pursuing independence.

Scotland and the United Kingdom make a good analogy for explaining Catalonia and Spain to the world. If we look closely, we see that the United Kingdom and Spain have a fair number of things in common, for example, both were formed as unified states at the beginning of the 18th century and both are comprised of multiple nations.

Britain, for example, is formed of English, Scottish, Welsh, and Irish. It's interesting to see that the English—who were and still are the largest and most important nation in the United Kingdom—never renounced their own nationality in order to become British. In Spain, the story is quite different. The Castilians, who were the largest of the nations that constituted the Spanish State, after conquering the other Iberian nations and abolishing their laws, languages, and constitutions, established a process of *castilianization* of the new unified Spain. In the end, they divvied up their own nation, Castile, and converted it into Spanish regions. They eventually stopped thinking of Castile as a nation and considered only Spain instead.

The English, on the other hand, have always kept their own identity, which has facilitated maintaining a relatively healthy relationship with their neighbors. In contrast, Spain has been trying to implement an aggressive program of "Spanishization" or *castilianization* of the Catalans, Basques, Galicians, and all other non-Castilians.

For that reason, the proposal of making Scotland an independent state from the United Kingdom has not raised such visceral hackles among the English, who understand it to be a Scottish affair. The English realize that an independent Scotland might fragment the United Kingdom but that its own nation, England, would remain intact. In Spain, the reaction is quite different. Since the Castilians are now only Spanish, they believe that an independent Catalonia would break up their nation. Therefore, the Spanish Government and Parliament have actively moved against any sort of recognition of the national identity of Catalonia even though it is well known that Catalonia was a nation well before Spain was created and, obviously, long before Castile was divided up.

The Spanish case is paradoxical. On the one hand it is a democratic country that belongs to the European Union of the 21st century. On the other, it is a state that, in contrast with the United Kingdom and Scotland, or Canada and Québec, has yet to recognize the status of "nationhood" for Catalonia, even though such status was passed by 90 per cent of the Members of the Catalan Parliament and ratified in a referendum by the Catalan people in 2006.

In fact, we can even go further. In contrast with Canada, and in the United Kingdom in particular—where each and every one of the Prime Ministers from Margaret Thatcher to David Cameron, including Tony Blair, have always recognized the right of the Scots to decide if they want Scotland to become an independent state—the Spanish government refuses to recognize this right to the Catalans, the Basques, or anyone else who asks for it.

Actually, the Spanish government has already announced that if the Catalan President goes ahead with the referendum in 2014, he will have to face the courts.

The Catalan businessman and engineer, Xavier Roig, once said that the United Kingdom, in contrast with Spain, is a country that knows how to spell "democracy". The prestigious columnist of the British daily *The Times*, Matthew Parris, who, it should be noted, was a conservative Member of Parliament in Westminster and who has spoken out against the independence of Catalonia, wrote this at the end of December 2012:

> *"If (Spanish) Prime Minister Mariano Rajoy and his bull-necked Partido Popular henchmen were put in charge of maintaining the unity of our own United Kingdom then within days we'd have the Armed Forces mobilised to storm the Scottish Parliament, Whitehall departments countermanding devolved legislation, Mr. Salmond carried shoulder-high to cheers down Edinburgh's Royal Mile, and soaring Scottish support for full independence."*

For the time being, it is fair to say that the most important difference between Scotland and Catalonia is that Spain is not the United Kingdom. On October 12, 2012, the UK's Prime Minister, David Cameron, and the Scottish First Minister, Alex Salmond, signed the "Edinburgh Agreement" in which both governments committed themselves to work together so that they can carry out the referendum on Scottish independence in 2014.

Interestingly enough, this agreement ended with a clause worthy of being mentioned:

> *"They [the UK and the Scottish Governments] look forward to a referendum that is legal and fair producing a decisive and respected outcome. The two governments are committed to continue to work together constructively in the light of the outcome, whatever it is, in the best interests of the people of Scotland and of the rest of the United Kingdom."*

Unfortunately in Spain, Catalans are not currently allowed to decide freely and democratically the future of our own country.

It is always a good time to recall the Declaration of Independence of the United States of America. Its second paragraph states:

> *"... all men are created equal, that they are endowed by their Creator with certain unalienable Rights, that among these are Life, Liberty and the pursuit of Happiness. —That to secure these rights, Governments are instituted among Men, deriving their just powers from the consent of the governed, —That whenever any Form of Government becomes destructive of these ends, it is the Right of the People to alter or to abolish it, and to institute new Government, laying its foundation on such principles and organizing its powers in such form, as to them shall seem most likely to effect their Safety and Happiness".*

It is a paragraph full of sensible and universal values that make us think that we are in the right.

Language in education

Miquel Strubell

Degrees in psychology from Oxford, London and Barcelona. After working 19 years for the Catalan government in the promotion of the Catalan language, he moved to the Open University of Catalonia in 1999, where his field is sociolinguistics and language planning. He has done research in the fields of minority languages, European language policy and the promotion of Catalan, and has coordinated a number of European projects and reports. He is a co-founder of the Catalan National Assembly.

A few months ago the chair in Multilingualism and the School of Psychology and Educational Science of the Open Catalan University[1] jointly published a booklet drawing together empirical evidence on linguistic attainment (in both Catalan and Spanish) and general academic attainment of schoolchildren in Catalonia attending the country's public schools. The booklet has also been translated into English as *Results of the Language Model Adopted by Schools in Catalonia: The Empirical Evidence.*[2]

Without a shadow of a doubt, given the social imbalance of Catalan and Spanish (the latter have encroached in many ways into Catalan society, as well as into the Balearic Islands and traditional Catalan-speaking areas in Valencia), schools are the only means at the disposal of democratic governments for achieving a fully bilingual and biliterate school-leaving population. However, different models are applied in different regions. In Valencia, the fact that a high proportion of youngsters (almost half, in fact) end their schooling without having a command of both official languages cannot but be interpreted as a failure of the model applied in that region[3]. Data from a large survey conducted in 2010 reveal an improvement, but in the youngest group, aged 15–24 years, those who claimed to speak the language "perfectly" or "quite well" only accounted for 57 percent of the age group.[4]

Why is the figure in Catalonia (85 percent) so much higher?[5] The simple answer is that in Valencia schools are segregated on linguistic grounds, which leads to a high proportion of pupils receiving insufficient instruction in Catalan and a deficient level of competency. Whereas in Catalonia a "linguistic conjunction" model is followed, meaning that all pupils attend schools with a broadly similar language-in-education model with regard to the use of Catalan as a medium of instruction. This model is geared to ensure social cohesion and to avoid substantial sectors of the school population finishing their education without a good command of Catalan, one of the official languages. It has enjoyed the longstanding (over 20 years) support of the great majority

---

1 http://www.uoc.edu

2 http://www.uoc.edu/portal/en/catedra_multilinguisme/index.html It was edited by Miquel Strubell, Llorenç Andreu, and Elena Sintes, and the contributions were by leading academics specialized in the field: Melina Aparici, Joaquim Arnau, Aurora Bel, Montserrat Cortès-Colomé, Carme Pérez Vidal, and Ignasi Vila.

3 See http://www.ub.edu/slc/socio/situacioactualcatala.pdf, page 3, for 2003–2004 comparative data

4 http://www.cefe.gva.es/polin/docs/sies_docs/encuesta2010/A4en.pdf

5 http://www20.gencat.cat/docs/Llengcat/Documents/Dades_territori_poblacio/Altres/Arxius/EULP2008.pdf (Table 7.2, p. 140).

of MPs represented in the Catalan Parliament as well as laudatory comments by the committee of Experts responsible for monitoring the application of the European Charter for Regional or Minority Languages. Thus in its report dated 21 September 2005 it stated that:

". . . the Committee of Experts observes that this system points to an impressive reversal of the trend. A regional/minority language that was still oppressed just 30 years ago has become the default language in the educational system in its traditional territory and the first language of instruction for the larger part of the last generation of young people who have been educated in Catalonia. Such a development is extremely rare in Europe's history and confirms the special interest of Spain in this domain."[6]

Any legal initiative aimed at improving the quality might therefore be expected to encourage the generalization of the most successful model. However, in these regions there are some parents who would like their children to opt out of being educated chiefly in the territorial language (even at the expense of equity in terms of outcomes). They have taken the issue to court on a number of occasions, demanding more than the initial schooling in Spanish that Catalonia's law has permitted since 1983. The vociferous calls of a few such families in Catalonia, generally not of longstanding Catalan origin, have been taken up by the Spanish conservative government—widely seen in Catalonia and the Basque Country as being run by a Spanish nationalist party—which has just caused a major public outcry in these two regions at least, by proposing a bill[7] which would effectively smash the current model, and relegate Catalan (and Basque and Galician) to the status, in evaluation terms, of foreign languages.

Coming in the aftermath of the Catalan elections, in which pro-independence parties won an outright majority and the Spanish conservative party came in a dismal fourth, the bill (which makes several clear references to the Catalan case without actually citing it) is being widely regarded as a further provocation and a new example of a policy of recentralizing power in Madrid.

---

6 http://www.coe.int/t/dg4/education/minlang/Report/EvaluationReports/SpainECRML1_en.pdf, paragraph 208

7 http://www.fe.ccoo.es/comunes/recursos/25/1443884-Ver_texto_del_Anteproyecto.pdf

What happened on November 25?

Pau Canaleta

Political, institutional, and business communications consultant. Political campaign communications strategist and communications advisor for large institutions, organizations, and businesses. Professor of communication at various universities, and speaker on electoral campaigns, brand positioning, institutional marketing, and storytelling. Author of books on political communication: L'estratègia electoral [Electoral Strategies] *and* Explica't amb una història [Tell Your Story with a Story], *Ed. UOC and* 100 días, 1 imagen [100 days, 1 Image] *Ed. Episteme. Canaleta holds undergraduate degrees in history, European studies, and a Masters in political marketing.*

On Sunday, November 25, 2012, the most important elections in Catalonia's recent history were held. The high turnout achieved—69.54 percent—confirms it.

It was an important election. For the first time, the whole Catalan nationalism movement—the bulk of the Catalan political system—had opted for a path toward separation. Never before had they opted for a separation between Catalonia and the rest of Spain.

It's not a coincidence that it was just at this moment that a significant part of the Catalan society made this choice. Spain's complete misunderstanding of Catalonia's personality, the fiscal plundering, the financial crisis, and above all, the ruling on the Catalan Statute of Autonomy has, gradually but surprisingly quickly, made for a shift in the arena of nationalist politics, from nationalism to sovereigntism, and from sovereigntism to independentism.

It wasn't, therefore, a process led by political parties, but rather by people who led this shift. In other words, it was the parties who were dragged by an nonsectarian independentist movement that threatened to transform the traditional party system of Catalonia that had been in existence since the Transition.

The demonstration on September 11, 2012 in which masses of people flooded Barcelona like never seen before, demanding independence, was the clearest and most visual proof of this political sea change. This was a demonstration that had the party leaders shaking in their boots thanks to the massive amounts of people, the unequivocal message that brought them together, and the diversity of the demonstrators.

The overwhelming evidence—the polls, movements, and declarations between cultural groups, associations, and business groups—made it clear that this wasn't just a cyclical change but something structural that the political parties would have to figure out how to respond to, in order to successfully channel it. If not, a big part of the population was going to walk right over them.

In the middle of all this, on September 20, there was a meeting scheduled at Moncloa—the Spanish "White House"—the very first meeting between the president of Catalonia and the president of Spain. In fact, this was the very first official reception of the Catalan president since Mariano Rajoy's electoral victory of November 20, 2011.

Artur Mas went to Madrid to fulfill his principal election promise with which he had definitively won the elections in 2010: a more fair fiscal pact for Catalonia that would reduce the fiscal plundering and that would improve the Catalan Government's cash flow, but above all, relieve the fiscal and financial pressure that Catalonia was (and is) suffering, which had become much more obvious under the current financial crisis.

Mas knew that he had the backing of a majority of Catalan society and that the people were closely watching the outcome of this meeting. After the demonstration of nationalist strength, Artur Mas could not return to Catalonia without achieving some of the demands expressed during the march. Otherwise, he would be obliged to raise his voice and attempt to lead the popular demands.

And that's how it went. After President Rajoy slammed the door on any possibilities for a fiscal pact, Artur Mas dissolved the Parliament and called early elections for November 25, 2012. The national transition had begun and now, the people of Catalonia had the possibility of deciding and clarifying exactly what they wanted. The elections took on an air of a plebiscite, thanks to the leadership of President Mas and his call to winning a decisive majority in order to begin a process of national emancipation.

So, what happened on Sunday, November 25, 2012?

The results surprised everyone. Convergència i Unió, President Mas' party, the predominant party in Catalan elections, won once more. However, it suffered a serious setback with regard to the number of seats, going from 62 to 50—where the absolute majority is 68 seats—and in the number of votes, losing 90,000, despite a turnout which was much higher than in previous elections, by about 10 points.

The traditional opposition party, the PSC (Partit dels Socialistes de Catalunya, Catalan Socialists Party, affiliated with the Spanish Socialist Party) suffered big losses, losing eight seats as well as second place in the Parliament.

ERC (Esquerra Republicana de Catalunya, the Pro-independence Catalan Left) had a great night, more than doubling its seats, going from 11 to 21 and becoming the second largest party in Parliament, as well as becoming the key to the governability of the country.

The PP (Partit Popular, or People's Party), the party of Spanish president Rajoy, gained a single seat and became the fourth strongest group in the Catalan Parliament, at a moment when in Spain, it enjoys a comfortable absolute majority.

The ecosocialists of ICV (Iniciativa per Catalunya Verds, or Initiative for Catalonia Greens) had good results, winning three new seats, basically from the socialists. This increase, however, did not give them any increased leverage in such a divided Parliament.

The other surprises of the night of November 25 were C's (Ciutadans or Citizens Party of the Citizenry) and the CUP (Popular Unity Candidates).

The first, which offered a clearly pro-Spanish campaign that was very critical with the current political class tripled its results winning nine seats and its own parliamentary group. The pro-Spanish campaign and its wide coverage in Spanish media made C's the clear winners of this election and handed them a significant portion of the pro-Spanish vote and those critical of the so-called political class.

The emergence of the CUP, with three seats, was another new element in these elections. Their campaign was pro-independence, revolutionary, and openly anti-system, and they were able to attract pro-independence voters as well as new voters who are very critical of the current political environment.

One of the more important aspects of the November 25 elections was the high turnout, much higher than normal in Catalan elections (around 60 percent) and comparable to any confrontation in the Spanish sphere. This was clearly due to the importance of these elections, that were perceived as vital to the electorate and that were closely and widely covered by the media, which seemed to enjoy this campaign, in all its peculiarities. And not so much by the Catalan media, which offered coverage similar to other electoral races, but by the Spanish media which, due to importance of the election, covered the election as much as they usually do the "national" ones. This favored the creation of an "electoral climate" especially among voters who only get their news through Spanish media. We can confidently state that in these elections, both those in favor and those against independence, and all those in between, came out to vote.

Within the sovereigntist groups, there was a displacement of votes from CiU to ERC—which has been seen since the CiU-PP pact of 2000 and doesn't seem to be going away—probably provoked by the budget cuts that President Mas' government had to implement during the two years of the legislature and which have been the harshest in all of Spain. This fact, together with the perception that Mas was very close to winning an absolute majority, and the authenticity of the pro-independence message of ERC's candidate, Oriol Junqueras, shifted an important number of voters that go back and forth between the two parties toward the latter candidate.

In the Barcelona metropolitan area—which contains the largest concentration of Catalonia's population as well as a significant portion of those who are descendants of immigrants from the rest of Spain, and thus traditional voters of Spain-wide parties like PSC and PP—CiU suffered important losses. This time, they lost a fair part of the "borrowed votes" that they had received in 2010 in order to finish off the unpopular leftist government that had governed Catalonia between 2003 and 2010. These then were voters who didn't agree with the pro-independence tack CiU had taken since September 11. Many of these voters divided themselves between other non-nationalist options: C's, PP, and PSC.

The Socialist Party of Catalonia also suffered losses, thanks to the dynamic between Socialist parties on a European level and the difficulties they've had telling their story and showing leadership in Catalonia. Even so, they did better than expected, thanks to the increased turnout in traditionally "socialist" areas. Despite that fact, the results were disheartening, taking into account the role that they've traditionally played.

The rest of the parties either had expected results or results foretold by the polls.

The principal takeaway was that even with the high turnout, the sovereigntist block maintained its weight and thus its advantage. There was a suspicion that a "Spanish elections" level turnout would favor the badly defined "unionists", but that simply did not happen. The sovereigntist advantage was clear and solid despite the high turnout. However, it's also true that it was the CUP that helped to maintain this advantage since it is a pro-independence party and probably responsible for a considerable number of the 500,000 new voters. The majority of these new voters—who don't usually vote in Catalan elections but who came out this time—were in favor of remaining with Spain, though the difference wasn't as big as it might have been because of the CUP.

We find ourselves then with a complex Parliament in which the will of the people has not been as clear as was thought. There is a clear nationalist majority in favor of nation building—including the first and second parties in Parliament—but with a somewhat weakened leadership. A joint majority requires those two pro-sovereignty parties—CiU and ERC—to work together for the first time toward a sovereign state.

Politics will be more important than ever. The country has voted for national transition, perhaps tenuously, and that the parties come together with agreements and pacts on the road to achieving it. Agreements between the parties will be essential.

Americans ♥ Catalonia: A geometric progression

Mary Ann Newman

Has been working in the field of Catalan literature and culture in the United States since the 1980s. She is a writer and translator who has published translations into English of novels and short stories by Quim Monzó and essays by Xavier Rubert de Ventós. She is currently translating Private Lives *by Josep Maria de Sagarra. She was awarded the Creu de Sant Jordi in 1998.*

The evening of February 23, 1981, I left the *Biblioteca de Catalunya* on my way to the Bar Almirall (a daily routine) and stopped at a kiosk to buy cigarettes (it was the eighties, after all). The radio was on, and I was horrified to learn that the Spanish Congress of Deputies was under attack. It must have been one of the last reports to come over Spanish radio, soon to be replaced by military or classical music, but a friend and I spent the night listening to the BBC on his shortwave radio. We were witnessing an attempt at a coup d'état by the Civil Guard. In the early morning, it was disarmed, but it would soon be clear that there had been a tectonic shift in the political landscape.

What had brought me there, in September 1980, was a Fulbright fellowship to do doctoral research in Catalan literature in Barcelona. In mid--semester, the Cultural Attaché at the American embassy in Madrid had come to town to get to know the Fulbright fellows, and invited us to lunch at a fine restaurant. There were twelve of us in Barcelona, but only two were working on specifically Catalan topics. The following day the attaché telephoned me with an astonishing proposal: "I want to support the Spain of the Autonomies, and I think one way of doing it is to establish university exchange programs. Would like to help me out in Catalonia?"

Would I ever. And it appeared the fates were with us. In February 1981, Representative John Brademas, swept out of Congress on Reagan's coattails, was to be installed as president of New York University (where I was doing my doctorate). Dr. Brademas had, to my surprise and delight, written a doctoral dissertation in the late 1950s on anarchism in Catalonia and Andalusia. Catalonia had an ally at the highest echelons of the university.

But then, in February, Lt. Colonel Tejero made his coup attempt. I let the dust settle for about a month, and then got in touch once again with the cultural attaché. When I broached the question of a university exchange between the United States and Catalonia, he said, "Mary Ann, the time has passed to support the Spain of the Autonomies. Now we must support Spanish democracy."

I ran to share my woes with philosopher Xavier Rubert de Ventós, my Catalan thesis director and friend, and a founding fellow of NYU's New York Institute for the Humanities, established by Richard Sennett. His surprising response: He would speak with his childhood friend, Pasqual Maragall, the deputy mayor of Barcelona, who was soon to be mayor. Maragall also had a long relationship with New York, having done an M.A. in Economics at the New School for Social Research. And so the project was reborn as an agreement between the University of Barcelona and New York University with the support of Barcelona City Hall. President Brademas and Rector Badia i Margarit signed the accord in December 1982. The Càtedra Barcelona-Nova York was born in September 1983. And I took a place in the watchtower of Catalan culture in the United States.

In those days, American awareness of Catalonia and Catalan culture was limited to scholars like Brademas, or Robert Burns, S.J., or Paul Freedman, historians. Or, to art historians like Edward Sullivan, and, just starting out, Robert Lubar (a brilliant scholar who learned perfect Catalan in the Catalan Studies program as he did his dissertation on Joan Miró). Or a devoted group of professors in Hispanic studies who founded the North American Catalan Society (in 1978!) and carried the language and literature wherever their academic careers took them. Or to lovers of opera and classical music, who followed the careers of Montserrat Caballé, Joan Pons, Josep Carreras, Alícia de Larrocha, Victoria de los Ángeles. Catalan culture was highbrow culture, the province of the happy few.

Yet, many people did not yet make the distinction between these artists as Catalans or as Spaniards. These were the years in which the "Catalans Universals"—Casals, Dalí, Caballé, Gaudí, and company—were celebrated in Catalonia, but were largely hidden behind the rubric "Spanish" in American museums and concert halls. They were, indeed, universal figures, but not necessarily as Catalans.

Progress in this regard has been gradual, but in time harbingers of change began to appear. The 1992 Barcelona Olympics drew new attention toward the beautiful Catalan capital—but not always toward Catalonia. Non-stop flights between New York and Barcelona started up. Barcelona took its logical, geographical place as the first or last port of call on Mediterranean cruises, and guidebooks and lectures reflected its cultural specificity.

Back in the States cultural institutions were coming under the direction of a new generation of thinkers. I once asked Richard Peña, director of the Lincoln Center Film Society, why he had decided in 2006 to mount a retrospective on Catalan film spanning the 20th century, and he responded: "I've always been interested in the stories that lay hidden under the official histories." This sensibility for the uncharted areas of world culture found support from newly established Catalan cultural institutions, the Institut Català d'Indústries Culturals, founded in 2000, and the Institut Ramon Llull, founded in 2002, while the disciples of previous generations of Catalan scholars were also taking their places at the helm of cultural institutions.

Not everyone has come up through the ranks. William Robinson, for example, the curator of modern European art at the Cleveland Museum, went to Barcelona to study a painting from Picasso's blue period and discovered an entire artistic tradition. The hidden treasure of Catalan art so captivated him that he spent the next seven years developing the major exhibition, "Barcelona and Modernity: From Gaudí to Dalí", which showed first at the Cleveland Museum in 2006 and then at the Metropolitan Museum in New York in 2007, drawing 475,000 visitors at the latter.

The audience was expanding, but it was still just the happy few. The next field to engage Americans was not art or music (where Jordi Savall and Montserrat Figueras were making their mark), but food. Catalan cuisine exploded into American consciousness in 2003 when Ferran Adrià graced the cover of the Sunday *New York Times Magazine*. From then on, no article on food trends was complete without a mention of Adrià or Catalan cuisine. And superb writers such as Francine Prose traveled off-season to Cadaqués, Pals and Empúries (the ancient Greek trading post on the Costa Brava) and reported on their travels and meals.

Still haute culture and haute cuisine, though. Yet the next frontier approached: Catalan athletes were showing up on the U.S. radar. Rafael Nadal from Mallorca became more and more popular on the U.S. tennis circuit. Pau Gasol was the first in basketball, with the Grizzlies, then the Lakers. His brother, Marc, soon followed, and then Ricky Rubio.

Sadly, American sports fans seemed impermeable to soccer, where Catalonia was legendary. This changed, though, with the 2010 World Cup. Soccer fever took hold. On the East Coast, sports bars opened at 8:00 a.m., offering breakfast so fans could watch the games. As Spain rose in the rankings, finally to take the Cup, US sportswriters took care to emphasize that eight of the eleven players were the product of La Masia, that is, the Barcelona Football Club, el *Barça*. (Even as I write this, *60 Minutes* is doing a full-length segment on the Barça. Who would have thought it?)

Catalan culture, in the broadest sense, was finally having its day. Then, the unimaginable happened. Catalonia became front page news, no longer relegated to the supplements, be they culture or sport. The Spanish debt crisis forced U.S. journalists to scramble to understand why tensions were exacerbated between the Catalan and Spanish governments. Catalonia has become hard news.

For some years, observers of the presence of Catalonia in the foreign press had noticed with concern that American journalists almost always deferred to the Spanish, not the Catalan, point of view in any given situation. A group formed to confront this imbalance: the Col·lectiu Emma. This tough collective of economists and professionals began proactively approaching journalists, countering mis- and dis-information, offering statistics and facts, and presenting the Catalan point of view on the issues.

So the terrain was prepared. The "crisis", paradoxically, has contributed to the positive presence of Catalonia in the news. Now, day after day, the *New York Times*, the *Chicago Tribune*, the *LA Times*, the *Wall Street Journal*, CNN, Bloomberg, ABC.com, and so on, feature intelligent, evenhanded articles on the Catalan situation.

To top it all, on September 11, Catalonia's National Day, a massive demonstration took place—1.5 million people, in a country of 7.5 million—in favor of the right of Catalans to decide their future relationship to Spain. That beautiful, peaceful expression of democratic sentiment, crowned by Catalan flags, captured the imagination of the American press (not so the Spanish press, which buried it at the bottom of the hour and fudged the numbers). The crisis is no longer just a crisis; it has become a cause.

A cause that is not difficult for Americans to understand, with our own history of separations and civil and cultural rights. After thirty years in the watchtower—which qualifies me as an old Catalan hand—it is gratifying to think that now not every conversation will have to start from scratch with the explanation that Catalonia is a region of Spain with its own language and literature. Finally, we can cut to the chase.

The viability of Catalonia as a state

Núria Bosch

B.A. and Ph.D. in Economics from the University of Barcelona. Bosch is professor of Public Economics at the same university, director of the UB's Chair in Fiscal Federalism at the Barcelona Institute of Economics (IEB) and one of the directors of the Fiscal Federalism Research Program at the same institute. The Barcelona Economics Institute is UB's research center that carries out work in Applied Economics. She specializes in fiscal federalism, local and regional public finance, fiscal flows, and public sector efficiency analysis. Her work has been published in specialized national and international journals and books.

Catalonia suffers from a significant fiscal drainage toward Spain in the form of a large fiscal deficit. This is the difference between the central government's public sector spending in Catalonia and the resources extracted from this community, mainly through taxation, by the central government.

Fiscal deficit data, all calculated using the same methodology, are available for 1986 until 2009 (Table 1). The average for 1986–2009 is 8 percent of GDP with a standard deviation around this average of only 0.9. Therefore, one can clearly speak of a structural fiscal deficit that affects the Catalan economy recurrently.

Table 1: Catalan fiscal deficit

	Million Euros	Percent of Catalan GDP		Million Euros	Percent of Catalan GDP
1986	- 2,465	- 6.7	1998	- 6,813	- 6.7
1987	- 2,868	- 6.9	1999	- 8,124	- 7.4
1988	- 3,466	- 7.4	2000	- 8,532	- 7.2
1989	- 4,056	- 7.6	2001	- 8,565	- 6.7
1990	- 4,867	- 8.2	2002	- 13,696	- 10.0
1991	- 5,174	- 7.9	2003	- 13,036	- 8.9
1992	- 5,988	- 8.5	2004	- 13,595	- 8.6
1993	- 7,263	- 10.0	2005	- 14,186	- 8.3
1994	- 6,732	- 8.7	2006	- 14,493	- 7.9
1995	- 6,416	- 7.6	2007	- 15,913	- 8.1
1996	- 7,088	- 7.8	2008	- 17,200	- 8.5
1997	- 7,018	- 7.3	2009	- 16,409	- 8.4
Average 1986–2009		- 8.0			
Standard deviation 1986–2009		0.9			

Source: Government of Catalonia.

Another way to understand this deficit drainage is to consider the fact that Catalonia contributes 19.5 percent to central government revenues via taxes and only receives 14 percent of central government spending, either in investment or other public services. These percentages are also the average for the period 1986–2009 and remain constant throughout those years.

Furthermore, we can note that although the fiscal deficit in terms of GDP remains more or less constant over time, it is not constant in terms of euros per inhabitant once the effect of inflation is removed. Between 1986 and 2009, the annual fiscal deficit for every Catalan has gone up from 1,076 to 2,251 euros. This is because the income of Catalonia has grown in real terms during this period.

This fiscal drainage is an important obstacle for the Catalan economy. It discourages growth and reduces Catalan well-being. The Spanish central government has historically refused to correct the problem. Catalonia has repeatedly tried to negotiate better fiscal treatment from the central government, but to date has not had any success.

I have recently analyzed what additional revenue Catalonia would have if it were an independent country and also what additional costs independence would incur. The analysis is for the period 2006–2009. My question is: what would have happened in this period if Catalonia had already been an independent state? I make two assumptions: first, I maintain the same level of taxation for these years, and second, I also maintain the same level of public spending and public services during this period.

Analyzing this period is particularly interesting because while 2006 and 2007 were still economic boom years, 2008 and particularly 2009 were years when the crisis had a significant impact on public finances.

Catalonia as an independent state would have received extra revenue of about 49 billion euros, which is an average over the period 2006–2009. These revenues would have come from the taxes that Catalans now pay to the Spanish central government. I should also mention that the current transfers from the Spanish central government to the Catalan government have been subtracted, as these transfers would disappear with secession.

On the other hand, an independent Catalonia would assume new responsibilities, which would mean more public spending. One of the most important would be the cost of Social Security (pensions and unemployment payments). It would also assume its own powers of state, such as foreign affairs (embassies), or the transfers that the Spanish government now makes to local governments. According to my calculations, the additional costs would have represented about 35 billion euros per year, this being the average for the period analyzed.

Therefore, the annual gain in revenue Catalonia would have received as an independent state would have been about 14 billion euros, which represents 7.1 percent of Catalan GDP. These resources could have been used to increase the level and quality of public services, to reduce taxes, and/or to narrow the current budget deficit of the Catalan government.

In conclusion, Catalonia's ability to finance itself as an independent state is undeniable. However, the reasons to ask for the Catalonia's secession are not only economic. There are other important reasons for independence, such as the continuous attacks of the Spanish central government against Catalonia's culture and language. Consequently, the only solution is Catalonia's secession from Spain. We hope we do not have to wait a long time to see Catalonia as an independent state.

To my Spanish friends

Salvador Garcia-Ruiz

B.A. in Economics from the Universitat Pompeu Fabra and an M.B.A. from the Stern School of Business at New York University. Garcia-Ruiz has been a consultant, an investment banker, and a film entrepreneur. He currently works in the education and research fields, and is an adjunct professor at Universitat Pompeu Fabra. He is the co-founder of the Col·lectiu Emma (Emma Network).

I lived for two years in Madrid. They were two of the best years of my life, especially the second one when Rosa came to live with me. Some of you I met there, and some I met in Barcelona, New York, London, and other places in the world. You already know—especially those of you who are on Facebook and Twitter—that I am an activist for independence, and I realize that some of you were surprised when you found out. Others were surprised and maybe hurt, but out of friendship or caution were hesitant to say anything to me about it.

I am in favor of independence, and I have been so for as long as I have had a political conscience, since I was 13 or 14 years old (even though I went to a religious school where most of the classes were given in Spanish with values that were a long way off from Catalanism!). I don't feel the way I do now because of the State's political hostility toward Catalonia, and I would feel the same way even if Catalonia had the highest possible level of self-government and respect within Spain. I simply want the country that feels like mine—Catalonia—to have the same recognition and rights as your country, Spain, does. I want Catalonia to be a normal country, nothing more, nothing less. In fact, I don't even consider myself a Catalan nationalist: just a Catalan. This concept is even hard for Catalan nationalists to understand. What I mean is that I consider myself Catalan in the same way that you consider yourself Spanish.

When I went to live in Madrid, I decided not to talk about politics. I didn't hide my pro-independence position when I was asked directly, but I didn't bring up the topic—Catalonia and its political situation—because I knew that it would only lead to arguments without much hope of reaching any consensus. I don't believe in educating people in Spain about Catalonia and given the results of those who do believe in it, time has proven me right. One of the few exceptions that I made was speaking with Luis A., one of my best friends. I told him all these things about Catalonia, about the Catalan language, and about independence, and he listened, but I don't think he understood. Still, he respected me, and that was what was more important.

As I told you, full disclosure, I am an independentist and I would be one even if Catalonia somehow managed to achieve a high level of self-government. But you have to understand that the growth of independentism is not among people who think like me, but with people who used to want—and tried, and dreamed of—finding a place for Catalonia within Spain. They have finally realized that it's not possible. I think the mistake was theirs. They wanted Catalonia to collect its own taxes, to have official sports teams, for the Catalan language to have official status in the European Parliament, for Catalonia to hold a seat on the Council of European Ministers . . . that is, they wanted it to be an independent state without being an independent state. That just doesn't exist in this world. And it sure doesn't exist within Spain.

There was an attempt to reform the law that regulates our self-government, the Statute of Autonomy, but it didn't come to anything, except to make Catalans even more frustrated. We followed the rules of the game. We got the Statute passed in the Catalan Parliament, in the Spanish Congress and Senate, and in a popular referendum . . . and then even though they had already "whittled it down" as Alfonso Guerra, a high level leader of the Spanish Socialist Party had boasted, the Constitutional Court finished it off by taking out some of its most important provisions. This was a turning point for a lot of people. And what happened over the next two years added insult to injury and pushed people to a point of no return with respect to their attitude toward Spain: "They don't care about us, it's better if we leave."

That's not all. We could make a list of grievances, like the financial relationship between Catalonia and the State, the State's broken promises to Catalonia, the tying up in court and permanent attack on Catalan in the schools, the feeling that we Catalans are used by politicians to win votes, and so on. You probably won't agree with those arguments, and you'll offer others about the bad things that some of us Catalans do. And we won't be able to come to an agreement about anything except that our relationship—the relationship between Catalonia and Spain—doesn't work.

The pro-independence feeling has grown as a reaction, as a counterplay, which is a shame, but it's not going away. I was pro-independence before discovering that independence offered many advantages to Catalonia and that it was impossible for us to fit in Spain. But now, beyond mere feelings, it's clear that the rational choice is to be in favor of independence. In fact, if you were Catalan, you probably would be too, who knows? Many "very normal" Catalans, who are not the slightest bit radical, who until now wouldn't have defended independence, now see it as absolutely necessary. And that's how they've expressed themselves at the polls, with a majority who support the parties that are in favor of Catalonia becoming a new independent state, and that's probably what would happen in a referendum if we Catalans could vote freely (which would be normal in any democracy but which the Spanish State currently denies Catalonia).

We'll be good neighbors. What we have now doesn't work. Catalonia wants more self-government and Spain doesn't want more decentralization.

Why does Spain have to be the way Catalans want it to be? It doesn't make sense. Spain should be how the Spanish want it, more or less centralized, with its monarchy, its symbols, its priorities . . . and Catalonia should be how we Catalans want it. Each one in its own way without imposing on the other.

It's a shame that the Spanish voices against Catalan independence that reach us are almost always threatening. Even Catalans who legitimately oppose independence feel angry about the arguments that are used outside of Catalonia to reject it. I would have liked to have heard an argument like "we want you to stay because we love you". Or even better: "Tell us how what you want to be and we hope you choose to stay with us." Whatever. What we have to try, at any rate, is to defend our own projects (independence in my case, and I don't know what in yours—that Catalans have a chance to decide? or a rejection of independence?) without disrespecting the other's. I want you to know that my pro-independence position is not based on being anti-Spanish, but rather on simply being Catalan. And I would like it if opposition to independence were not based on political, judicial, or military threats. This last bit worries me a lot.

I wanted to write this note in order (to try) to explain to you what's going on in Catalonia and how I'm living it. It's complicated and I hope the note has served its purpose. In any case, I don't ask that you understand it, just that you respect it.

We'll be good neighbors. The truth is today, outside of politics, we're already good friends.

Best,

Salva

The Catalan business model

Joan Canadell

General Secretary of the Cercle Català de Negocis (Catalan Business Circle)

For centuries, Catalonia has been an industrially dynamic territory, graced with modernism and development. Mediterranean commerce has always been bustling thanks to the business corridors along the Mediterranean Coast and indeed along the whole coast of Southern Europe. As long ago as the 13th-century Catalonia has enjoyed moments of stunning commercial success driven by the astute development of whatever advance corresponded to the era, culminating in the 18th-century Industrial Revolution, which in Catalonia remarkably took place despite the absence of coal, and instead smartly took advantage of the driving force of the Catalan rivers to give birth to numerous industries all over the Catalan lands.

During the 20th century, Catalonia was recognized as the factory of Spain, but in fact, we can show that the Catalan Nation has always been the business and industry axis around which Spain has prospered. This is our tradition, passed down from our parents, grandparents, and great-grandparents. Regardless of where we came from, through numerous waves of immigration, this has been a land of creative and innovative business and commercial entrepreneurs.

It has only been in the last 15 to 20 years that Catalonia has lost a part of its business leadership to other autonomous communities, especially Madrid, thanks to the continual, unbalanced, and favored treatment that the Spanish government offers the centralized model of administration and economics. There are many examples, of which we'll cite just a few: the strict radiality of the network of high-speed trains and highways that all pass through Madrid, the artificial supports and promotion of Terminal T4 in Madrid's Barajas airport, or the driving of multinational headquarters closer to the Madridian power hub.

The Spanish economic model of the nineties was based on supporting huge companies, which many times were privatized but directed by "friends" of the powers-that-be, all of which were centralized in Madrid, and grew, thanks to State support that never demanded that these companies be competitive, as long as they wielded political control. These are the companies that grew thanks to huge profits derived from the oversized investments in public works that were undertaken without any reasoned economic planning in most cases, and which set the stage for massive accumulated public debt. Airports without airplanes, highways without cars, and high-speed rail without passengers are all a part of the this model's legacy, which has chiefly benefited the huge construction companies, banks, and service companies, as well as the politicians who have profited from the indirect gains of the big business earnings.

This is the Spanish economic model, but not the traditional Catalan one, which in contrast is one of small and medium-sized businesses (which represent 99 percent of the business landscape). There are a few large Catalan businesses as well, which are leaders in various productive sectors, such as food, pharmaceutical, metallurgical, automobile, chemical, services, tourism, and so many others. We can say without a doubt that Catalonia is one of the most varied of the industrial regions in Southern Europe. The numbers speak for themselves: with 6 percent of the geographic territory of the Spanish State, Catalonia makes up 16 percent of the population, 20 percent of the Gross Domestic Product, 24 percent of the industry, 26 percent of the exports, and 31 percent of the middle and high-valued technology exports.

But Catalonia is also a clear leader in tourism. It is the number one cruise liner port of Europe and fifth in the world. World-famous Barcelona is one of its most important brands. It hosted a model Olympic Games, and was and is the home of world-renowned modernism figures such as its ambassador Antoni Gaudí, famous painters Salvador Dalí, Joan Miró, and Pablo Picasso; world-famous chefs such as Ferran Adrià and Carme Ruscadella, and without a doubt, the best soccer team in history, recognized for a style of play that has revolutionized the sport.

The Catalan model has absolutely nothing in common with the Spanish or Greater Madridian model. Any strategic analysis would clearly reveal that developing these two models requires separate, very distinct game plans. It's obvious then that Spain doesn't have one problem, it has at least two. On the one hand, that of the dynamic economic regions like Catalonia, with a structured and creative network of small- and medium- sized businesses that need support so that they can focus even more on the global market and on developing with more R+D+i. And on the other hand, the historically nonindustrialized regions that have grown artificially in the last few years thanks to a model that cannot sustain them without a strong injection of external credit.

Given that the Catalan economic and business model cannot share the solutions that might be applied to a Spanish model, the conclusion is quite simple: we need to defend, promote, and internationalize our own model even more than we have been able to do so far. And that will only be possible with support from the State. Our own Catalan State.

The CUP: the oldest and newest independentists

Roger Buch i Ros

Ph.D. in Political Science from the Autonomous University of Barcelona. Expert in the history and current situation of pro-independence political parties. Currently professor at Ramon Llull University. Author of the books L'esquerra independentista avui [Today's Pro-Independence Left] *(Columna 2007) and* L'herència del PSAN [PSAN's legacy] *(Editorial Base 2012).*

On November 25, 2012, the elections to the Catalan Parliament were marked with independentist fervor. The Candidacies for Popular Unity (CUP), which was presenting itself for the first time in this kind of election, won three seats. It turns out these newest independentists who also have the support of the youngest voters are paradoxically the oldest pro-independence formation. Let's take a look back in history.

At the end of the 1970s, once General Franco's dictatorship was over and done with, Catalonia was trying on its new political autonomy amid the general euphoria of the Catalan people and a majority of political parties. Some smaller political groups, however, denounced the autonomous government and demanded independence for the Catalan Countries. They were revolutionaries who mirrored the decolonization struggles that had taken place years before in various countries across the world. These independentists were few in number and indeed were looked upon with a certain perplexity by the Catalanist movement, which was satisfied to try out the new political autonomy afforded it after years of Francoist darkness and prohibition of the Catalan language.

These small groups defended independence, the Catalan Countries, and socialism. They positioned themselves against the new laws, including the Spanish Constitution (1978) and the Statute of Autonomy of Catalonia (1979) that regulated the autonomous government of Catalonia, all the while demanding that a Catalan State be created. In addition, they were in favor of the Catalan Countries, that is, they claimed as the subjects of the future Catalan State the group of territories where Catalan is spoken. Not just Catalonia, but also the Valencian Country, the Balearic Islands, and Northern Catalonia within the French borders. Finally, they declared themselves in favor of a socialist state that would promote an egalitarian society along economic lines.

During the 30 years that passed between then and now, this area of radical leftist pro-independence has gone through many changes and mutations. On the one hand, there have been a series of microparties and organizations that have suffered the typical fragmentation of all extraparliamentary movements. They have stayed on the sidelines of the political system and at some points (during the eighties) encouraged confrontations on the street with the Spanish police and even supported armed propaganda groups. These groups were unable for many years to offer a political alternative and ended up essentially remaining a youth struggle movement specializing in propaganda campaigns on the street. While the independentist left was adept at attracting young people thanks to their radical image, many independentists decided to pass over to more moderate parties like ERC and ICV when they became adults.

As the years went by, the pro-independence left began to reconstruct itself and established a slew of organizations, always through the influx of youth members. Currently, there are groups like Endavant-OSAN, MDT, the youth organization Arran, or the Student Union of the Catalan Countries (SEPC), who have an important presence in the universities. One must also point out that there are numerous "pro-independence clubs", neighborhood meeting places that are very active and that host chats, campaigns, and general activism. Finally, after a long trip through the desert, the resurrection of historic independentism comes at the hand of the CUP group, which was initially used only to present candidates in municipal elections.

The CUP had for years been offering candidates to municipal elections and gaining a handful of council positions. They starting getting good results in 2003 and this increased significantly in 2007, and especially in 2011 when they won 100 municipal council seats, with many in important towns like Reus, Girona, Sant Cugat del Vallès, Mataró, Vilanova i la Geltrú, Vilafranca, Manresa, and Vic.

At the end of October 2012, in the midst of the euphoria shared with other independentist parties, thanks to the massive demonstration on September 11, 2012 (Catalonia's National Day), the CUP decided for the first time to present itself for the elections for the Parliament of Catalonia. They made the decision in open assembly just a few days before the deadline for signing up, since they were snap elections without a lot of advance notice.

They offered David Fernández at the head of the list for the electoral district of Barcelona. He is fairly well known among the alternative social movement sphere in Barcelona. The electoral campaign's slogan was "It's the people's moment" with a three-concept classic slogan of the movement: "Independence, Socialism, Catalan Countries". They spoke of "Total independence" not only with respect to Spain, but also with respect to the economic markets.

The CUP campaigned with a small budget, held together with the volunteer efforts of its members. They underscored the importance of social justice rather than independence. The latter was taken for granted, since who was more in favor of independence than they had been for 30 years? It's representative of the electoral campaign that their video #somunitatpopular [we are a united people] was the most shared video through social media in the entire Catalan electoral campaign. In that video, images appear from various protest movements: against foreclosure evictions, against excessive police action, against budget cuts to social services due to the economic crisis, and in defense of the rights of immigrants. It must be said that Barcelona and its environs have been an important greenhouse for alternative social movements. On the one hand, the antiglobalization movement at the beginning of the 2000s and on the other the one that more recently has been known as the "indignants" movement. The indignants, also known as #15M—since they filled the squares of Spain's principal cities on May 15th (2011)—demanded a new kind of politics that was closer to the people. The movement harshly criticized the democratic representative system, accused the political classes in general of taking advantage of their positions in order to get rich, and demanded a new relationship between the system and its citizens.

The CUP centered their very focused campaign on attracting the votes of this diffuse alternative left, many of the members of which don't explicitly identify with independentist demands.

On November 25th, the CUP surprised everyone by entering Parliament with 125,000 votes (3.48 percent of the total). They were awarded three seats in Barcelona and almost got a seat in Girona as well. In contrast with other independentist organizations whose vote was concentrated in rural areas, the CUP also received good percentages in the metropolitan areas, and in cities with less independentist tradition, a fact that supports the theory that they were able to attract at least a part of the "indignant" vote.

According to all sources, many of the CUP's votes came from people who had abstained from voting in previous elections. It's also important to point out that other parties who were most closely aligned with the CUP's ideology, such as ICV (eco-socialist and in favor of the right to self-determination) and ERC (moderate left independentists), also had improved results. It turns out that the sum of the votes for the three parties (3, 13, and 21 MPs, respectively) was much higher than the result that the principal leftist party in Catalonia—PSC, which is tied to PSOE and in favor of maintaining the relationship with Spain—had gotten up until that election.

The CUP is the heir of the old independentists, the more historic ones, but today independentism is not an important part of their identity, in contrast with 30 years ago, when many other parties were also independentist. What sets them apart has more to do with a possible new way of doing politics. They represent a phenomenon that is more like the uprising of the Greens in Germany at the beginning of the eighties or the current Pirate Party in some European countries like Sweden, or even to protest movements like

Occupy Wall Street (OWS) in the United States: radical democracy, defense of *assemblyism*, and critique of the traditional political class.

The day that the Parliament was constituted, the three new Members of Parliament from the CUP used several symbols to demonstrate that a new system of political representation was possible, a revolution in the way of acting with the aim of bringing politics closer to the people. One expects them to offer frontal opposition to the new CiU (center-right sovereigntist) government. There will be opposition in all areas except one, that of the referendum on independence, where presumably, even as they show their displeasure with the way the question is framed without including the Catalan Countries, they will support it. In the words of David Fernández, they will only be in agreement with CiU for a fraction of a second: at the moment they vote Yes in the referendum for the independence of Catalonia. In all other areas, the CUP promises to lead a policy of uncompromising opposition. We will be, they say, "the Trojan horse" of the working class in the Parliament. The anti-system movement has made it inside.

Our September 11th (1714)

Marta Rovira-Martínez

Ph.D. in Sociology from the Autonomous University of Barcelona. Rovira-Martínez researches identity, national symbols, immigration, and language in Catalonia. She has directed numerous projects, among them the documentary, Forjadors de la Diada [The Origin of Catalonia's National Day] *in collaboration with Enric Saurí. She has received the Jaume Camp Prize for Sociolinguistics in 2012 for her work on the linguistic integration of Spanish-speaking immigrants. In English, she has published* Rethinking migration policies *(IEMED-UNFPA, 2006) and the article "Multilingualism, an emerging value" (Noves SL Fall/Winter 2007)*

> *"We chose September 11, 1714 because it is the most important event in our history, the date on which the largest number of our people died in the name of freedom for our Country."*[1]
>
> Lluís Marsans, secretary of Catalanist Union, in an invitation to the 1901 demonstration

On September 11, 2001, the United States of America suffered the worst foreign attack in its history. That day, while Catalonia commemorated its National Day *(la Diada)*, everyone watched aghast as the images of the falling Twin Towers were projected around the world. We couldn't believe that it wasn't a movie. It was so shocking that it took us a while to understand what had happened. In New York, and throughout the United States, it must have been even harder to absorb such a tragedy.

On September 11, 1714, on the other hand, the Catalans immediately understood that the fall of Barcelona meant the end of their country. On that day Barcelona fell to the hands of the Bourbon armies after a siege that had lasted thirteen months. Catalonia suffered the worst defeat of its history. The subsequent chronicles tell of the ferocious oppression by the victorious forces, from which the Catalans would take years to recover. They had faced the powerful Spanish and French empires. And they had lost.

The loss of Catalan liberties

Until 1714, the Crown of Aragon (Catalonia, the Kingdoms of Valencia, Mallorca, and Aragon), together with the Crown of Castile formed a confederacy borne of the marriage in 1469 between Ferdinand and Isabella, the *Catholic Monarchs*. Catalonia and the other lands of the Crown of Aragon maintained their own Constitutions and their own political systems based on the idea of a pact between the monarch and the representatives of the people. In virtue of this pact, the king had to swear loyalty to the Constitutions in order to be recognized. When Charles II of Spain died in 1700 without an heir, the European monarchies declared war on each other to determine a successor. While Castile sided with Philip V, grandson of Louis XVI of France, Catalonia and the other territories of the Crown of Aragon threw their support behind Charles, Archduke of Austria (later Charles VI, Holy Roman Emperor).

---

1 Marsans, Lluís (1911). "Un recort, una defensa y un prec", *Renaixement* magazine. September 11, 1911. Under the pseudonym, A. Mallsol.

The loss of the war by Charles of Austria's allies led to the Treaty of Utrecht of 1713, in virtue of which the Bourbon Phillip V was proclaimed King of Spain. But the Catalans, who had initially received support from England and who believed they might still count on such aid, decided to continue the resistance against a monarchy that had no intention of respecting its Constitutions and liberties. Barcelona lasted thirteen months under a relentless, infernal siege. To try to imagine it, remember that more than 30,000 bombs fell on a city of less than 35,000 inhabitants.

After Phillip V won the war, he instituted an extremely harsh repression against the Catalans: the city was occupied by the military, new taxes were imposed, institutions were abolished, the language was persecuted, and the most bustling commercial center of the city was razed so that a fortified citadel could be erected in its place. The military officials were imprisoned, tortured, and killed. One of the most horrific cases was that of General Josep Moragas, who was tortured and then hung. His head was placed in a cage and dangled a few feet from the ground for twelve years. Four thousand people were detained, executed, deported, or given long sentences. All over Catalonia, castles and forts were demolished.[2] Thirty thousand people, mostly nobles and members of the ruling classes, exiled themselves in Vienna, under the protection of the Emperor Charles. The repression had a chilling effect on the economy, the culture, and the language of the Catalans such that the chroniclers of the era spoke of "the end of the Catalan nation". The aim of the Bourbons was precisely that: to erase the Catalan identity.

The commemoration of the *Diada*

But they were unsuccessful. The Catalans never forgot 1714 and, at the end of the 19th century, when romantic nationalist movements were breaking out all over Europe, in Catalonia too there was a renaissance of culture and initiatives in favor of increased political autonomy. It was then that acts in memory of the martyrs of the fall of Barcelona were celebrated by the community. In 1888, the statue of Rafael Casanova, the first councilor of the City of Barcelona during the siege of 1714, was inaugurated, and it was then that the ritual began of leaving flowers at its pedestal to honor the "martyrs of 1714", in addition to remembrance masses, poetic readings, and the singing of the Catalan national anthem.[3]

---

2 Albareda, Joaquim Salvadó i García Espuche, Albert (2005). *11 de setembre de 1714*. Generalitat de Catalunya.

3 Crexell, Joan (1985), *El monument a Rafael Casanova*. El llamp.

The repression by the Spanish authorities against these acts of homage organized by the community only served to give them an increasing significance as an act of resistance and of struggle for freedom. It is in this way that September 11 has become a day of commemoration and remembrance of those who fought for Catalonia's freedom. The *Diada* is a very important date in the Catalan calendar, which in addition marks the beginning of the school year and the end of summer vacation.

For Catalans, the national symbols are a very important aspect of civic and political life in Catalonia. They are so much so that the first law approved by the Parliament of Catalonia—once this institution was recovered after the Franco dictatorship—was the approval of the National Day, the national hymn, and the national flag of Catalonia.[4]

On September 11, the center of Barcelona fills with crowds. Families with young children, young people, old people, political and union leaders, guests of foreign organizations, and more. The city spills out onto the streets. Numerous activities take place in the same spaces of the old part of the city that were the protagonists in the siege of 1714. On the one hand there are the institutional events, and on the other, the events organized by a growing number of community organizations: booths that sell independentist flags, pins, books, and all sorts of other products, activities for kids and families, concerts, guided tours to historic places, and more. The balconies of the buildings, the streets, and even the buses are decorated with flags in quite a festive atmosphere.

The most relevant act is that which consists of bringing a crown of flowers to Rafael Casanova's statue. Since the Second Republic, and after the Franco era, the tradition dictates that the principal institutions of the country—the most important businesses (like the FC Barcelona Soccer club) and all of the associations who so choose—should bring their arrangement of flowers, normally decorated according to the coat of arms and symbols of each group. Each entity and institution that brings flowers to Casanova's statute also sings Catalonia's anthem—"The Reapers" *[Els segadors]*—to the statue.

Since 1913, there is also a ceremony for the fallen during the siege of Barcelona who were buried in the *Fossar de les Moreres* [the Mulberry Tree Pit], next to the dramatic, gothic, imposing Church of Santa Maria del Mar. Since 2001, in addition, there is a red wall in which are inscribed a few of

---

4 LLEI 1/1980, dated June 12, by which the National Day of Catalonia, September 11, is declared.

the most famous poetic verses written by Frederic Soler about the fall of Barcelona in 1714: *In the Mulberry Tree pit, no traitor is buried. Even though our flags were lost, it is still an urn of honor.* This is where the most radical patriotic associations still meet, because it is considered the space of the true heroes: the anonymous.

Since 2004, the Parliament of Catalonia holds its own ceremony which reflects celebrations that take place in free countries. The army does not take part, but there is a representation from the *Mossos d'Esquadra* (the local Catalan police force), in gala dress. Catalonia's national anthem is sung, and important cultural personalities take part. In 2009, the Israeli singer Noa was among them, attracting a large audience.

September 11 is also celebrated in all of the towns and smaller cities of Catalonia. In each one there is a monument or a place that commemorates the War of Succession and that serves as a focal point for paying homage to the dead from that war. In recent years, there have also been many people who participate in torch marches. The torches are used to symbolically burn the Decree of *Nova Planta* of 1716 that Phillip V approved in which Catalonia's liberties and Constitutions were abolished.

Since the seventies, the afternoon and evening of September 11 are given over to a march in favor of the independence of Catalonia. During the Spanish political Transition, these demands were clearly in the minority. Even though the Catalans wanted independence, many believed that it simply wasn't possible and that in the new Spanish democracy, Catalonia's situation would be acceptable enough. But as independentist feeling has grown, so has the number of participants in the march. During the seventies and eighties, the police would intervene at the end of the march, beating and detaining people. The next day's press would use the images of the clashes with the Spanish police to criminalize the commemoration.

Barcelona's September 11 marches

Catalans know, however, that September 11 is not just any date, and that marching on that date has a special significance. For that reason, it's not surprising that several especially important marches have taken place in Catalonia on that date. The first was in 1901, in response to the arrest of 23 young people by the Spanish police. That year therefore marks "the Day's popular awakening", according to the incisive words of Vicenç A. Ballester, who added, "24 hours of prison for a few, gave much to think about to many".

In 1976, shortly after the death of Franco, the organizations and political parties that formed the Assembly of Catalonia decided to organize a commemoration on September 11. But the civil governor of Barcelona, Sánchez Terán, decided it was too dangerous to let Catalan sentiment be so freely expressed. So he forced the celebration of September 11 that year to be celebrated outside of Barcelona. The organizers brought their commemoration to a nearby city, Sant Boi de Llobregat, where Rafael Casanova had been interred. Thousands of people went, making it the first massive organized act in Catalonia after Franco's death. The desire for freedom could not be stopped.

In 1977, right in the middle of the political Transition and with the community experiencing a deep awakening, Barcelona had one of the biggest marches in its history. About 1 million people paraded down the great avenues of the city. The demonstration was headed by the slogan "Liberty, Amnesty and Statute of Autonomy". In other words, democracy, amnesty for the political prisoners, and a regime of self-government for Catalonia within the framework of the Spanish State.

Thirty-five years later, in 2012, there was a march that was even larger than that of 1977. This time, there were 1.5 million people. The demonstration was called for 5 p.m. in the evening. But all day, on the roads and railways, you could see that there was a human tide that was coming into Barcelona. A happy feeling came over everyone: children, young people and old, entire families filling the streets without being able to take a single step forward because those streets were so full. There were Catalan speakers and Spanish speakers, immigrants from all over the world, Catalans of all stripes. The demonstration was a peaceful manifestation that gave hope to a Catalonia which no longer feels comfortable within Spain.

1714–2014: Will Catalonia triumph again?

It's important to keep in mind that the commemoration of September 11, 1714 has almost always been repressed by the Spanish authorities, especially by the dictatorships of Primo de Rivera (1923–1930) and Francisco Franco (1939–1975). During the Franco era, Rafael Casanova's statue was taken down and ordered to be destroyed, like many other monuments and symbols of the Catalan nation. But an employee of the Barcelona city government saved it by hiding it in a warehouse and covering it behind a sheetrock wall. Each September 11, the Francoist authorities prohibited people from even going near the place where the statue had been. But the Catalan resistors kept paying homage clandestinely, despite the difficulties and dangers.

Despite the repression, the commemorations did not disappear, and on the contrary, as years have passed, they have become more and more important. Even in democratic times, however, it has been a celebration looked on with scorn by Spanish nationalist parties with representation in Catalonia. And it has also been looked down upon by the Spanish authorities, who have tried to take away its symbolic value and to link it to the acts of a few radicals. However, the National Day of Catalonia is not a crazy act of a few radicals, but rather a heartfelt commemoration by a people who knows that it has the right to freedom.

The current political context, in which the majority are in favor of the independence of Catalonia, coincides with the preparations for the commemoration of the 300th anniversary of the end of the siege of 1714. Indeed, the revival of the National Day has gone hand in hand with the growth in independentist feeling among the people. The memory of 1714 is increasingly relevant as a symbolic presence. Since 2005, there have been various community groups and some city governments that have supported acts that commemorate various moments during the War of Succession. But because 2014 is so close the *Generalitat* (Catalan Government) and the Barcelona city government have begun to prepare for such an important commemoration and to treat the 300th anniversary with the proper solemnity. We will see if the proposal put forth by President Lluís Companys—executed by firing squad under Franco in 1940—comes to bear. He proclaimed, "We will suffer again, we will fight, and we will win."

Basic Bibliography

Albareda, Joaquim Salvadó i García Espuche, Albert (2005). *11 de setembre de 1714*. Generalitat de Catalunya.

Ballester, David. (2002) *El triomf de la memòria: la manifestació de l'Onze de Setembre de 1977.* Barcelona: Editorial Base.

Benet, J. I Espinàs, J.M. (1977). *El llibre de la Diada.* 11 Setembre 1977. Barcelona

Crexell, Joan (1985). *El monument a Rafael Casanova.* Barcelona

Fanés, Fèlix (1977) "L'onze de setembre sota el franquisme". *L'Avenç*, no. 5. Barcelona.

Riera, Sebastià (1994). *La commemoració de l'Onze de Setembre.* Barcelona: Ajuntament de Barcelona

Sobrequés, Jaume (1976). *L'Onze de Setembre i Catalunya.* Barcelona: Undarius.

Index

D

E

W

X

Made in the USA
Charleston, SC
16 March 2013